Practical Incident Management in K–12 Schools

Practical Incident Management in K–12 Schools

How Leaders Prepare for, Respond to, and Recover from Challenges

Brian N. Moore

ROWMAN & LITTLEFIELD
Lanham • Boulder • New York • London

Published by Rowman & Littlefield
A wholly owned subsidiary of The Rowman & Littlefield Publishing Group, Inc.
4501 Forbes Boulevard, Suite 200, Lanham, Maryland 20706
www.rowman.com

Unit A, Whitacre Mews, 26–34 Stannary Street, London SE11 4AB

British Library Cataloguing in Publication Information Available

Library of Congress Cataloging-in-Publication Data

978-1-4758-2677-7 (cloth : alk. paper)
978-1-4758-2678-4 (pbk. : alk. paper)
978-1-4758-2679-1 (electronic)

∞™ The paper used in this publication meets the minimum requirements of American National Standard for Information Sciences—Permanence of Paper for Printed Library Materials, ANSI/NISO Z39.48–1992.

Printed in the United States of America

Contents

Foreword

My kids love to go to school. I can remember well their first days at school, our excitement of those few first experiences followed by literally hundreds of other firsts as they learned new ideas and concepts. My wife Annie and I were thrilled with their education and how well all three of them did in school. Like most good parents, we also worried about them.

Anyone who has read a newspaper or watched television has heard stories about some incident or disaster that had an impact on a school. My heart felt for the families in Moore, Oklahoma when in 2013, a tornado devastated their small town during a school day. Literally hundreds of first responders and residents rushed to the elementary school that had been hit directly by the funnel cloud. The eyes of parents around the country if not the globe were fixed on this community as they slowly recovered and rescued each and every student in good health. Together, we breathed a universal sigh of relief.

My thoughts shifted during those days to my role as a United States Senator, and I began asking myself: "How can we help those schools to prepare for these types of emergencies?" How do we make sure that when our children go to school, that the school is as prepared to care for our children as we are?

In my time as an elected official in my home state of Delaware, I worked with our schools and public safety agencies to ensure that there were ample resources our schools could use to develop strong safety plans, when as New Castle County President and as County Executive, supporting the Police Athletic League with grants to support after school violence prevention programs for local school districts and working closely with the New Castle County Land Use department for physical security upgrades to schools.

As a nation, we constantly spend time preparing for and handling national crises and emergencies. I work with key federal agencies that focus their careers planning for the unplannable and thinking about the unthinkable. We all can rest assured that they are planning and preparing so that we can over-come the difficulties that could impact our country at any time.

It's a funny thing when you can apply the skills developed as a parent when you become Senator. When our children, Michael, Jack and Maggie were babies, we would look around the house for anything that could hurt them. We kid-proofed everything from sharp edges, to stairs and cabinets. Like any new parent, we worried about the worst that could happen. Now, I get to do it on a much larger scale. Instead of stairways and cabinets, I work with our partners to look at counties and states; different size but same concept.

The Federal Emergency Management Agency briefs Congress annually and is available to meet at our request, to discuss not only what the potential threats are to our country, but also how they would respond. Detailing the resources they have and how they would use them is a part of each brief. Like a good parent, they hope for the best but prepare for the worst.

Then, we look at our most vulnerable populations, those young children who come to school every day optimistic and eager for new learning experiences. They are not thinking about what would happen if there was a fire or if a tornado were to strike the school. Their teachers and principals are the ones who have to think about those "bad things." We need to look to experts like Brian who can help get us familiar with the things we need to know to protect those kids from those bad things.

With all of our legislation from the federal government and states down to the local school districts, we often look at requiring physical changes and buildings walls and fences and even locking doors differently, but we rarely look at training and changing the way we think about these things. Emergencies require educators to think differently, to put on a different hat. Brian has done a great job of helping every principal attain the knowledge he or she needs to be able to don the emergency managers' hat and wear it well.

Chris Coons
United States Senator (D-DE)

Acknowledgments

For more than a decade I have had the chance to work with literally hundreds of fantastic and hardworking school administrators around the country. Inevitably the discussion turned to emergency planning, my realm of expertise. What always impressed me was the desire that they all had to learn better ways to protect their students. It is the same zeal that they show for new techniques to teach children. Their dedication to the safety of their students is always a source of inspiration to me.

When Rowman & Littlefield asked me to write a book on emergency planning for schools, I thought it would be a great challenge and exciting chance to share what I think is a great tool for many different aspects of an administrator's life. I cannot thank Sarah Jubar enough for her guidance and advice from the concept of the book through the finished work. Without her effort this work would still be a few pages of notes.

I want to thank my friend and editor Pat George from ASBO International for all of her support for my writing for the past ten years. She has been a great inspiration, and I could only have done this because of her encouragement.

I am incredibly thankful to my kids, Brendan and Megan, for all of their support as their Dad hid in the dining room all those nights and weekends to write. None of this could have happened without the loving support of my wife Karen. After twenty years of her belief that I should write a book, here it is my love. Thanks for always believing in me!

I would like to dedicate this book to my mother-in-law Kathryn Fitzsimmons. Mom always told us to follow our dreams and follow our hearts. This one is for you, Mom.

Introduction

This book is broken down into sections that match up with the four phases of emergency management: mitigation, preparedness, response, and recovery followed by mitigation and preparedness again. In addition, there are sections that will help you to retain your newfound skillset as a successful incident manager. This is only the first page, so do not panic if you don't know a thing about the emergency management cycle—it is all in the book! Just as you will do with your new emergency plan, it all starts with planning and mitigation, so that is where the book will start.

Each chapter ends with a group of lessons learned. These are the key take-aways from each chapter and are there to help you remember what was really important. Mind you, they are lessons learned from years of experience as well as best practices following incidents in schools and other emergencies around the nation, if not the world.

One key is to read through the book first from beginning to end. While it may be tempting to go straight to the section on incident command and responding to emergencies, if you do not have the background information and the key tools to allow you to respond effectively, then the information in the response section will not be as valuable. (Since this text is designed for educators, remember that we teach addition and subtraction before we teach students binomials.)

After you read through and after you have had a chance to try out the incident command systems (ICS), use the book as a desk reference. Each year before school starts, review the sections again just to make sure that you and your team are ready for what comes next. If you need specific information, go right to the section and use the tools and graphics in the section to reinforce your knowledge. Unlike your colleagues in the emergency services, you may not use ICS every day, so a refresher now and again will be very helpful in keeping your skills sharp!

Section I

MITIGATION

Chapter 1

A Timeline for Disaster

HOW QUICKLY AN ISSUE BECOMES AN EMERGENCY

It began as a quiet fall day in a large high school on the East Coast. Nearly 600 students had come to school that morning and were settled nicely into their school day. Slowly they had begun to adapt to the new school year, no more questions about which class was next and which teacher was the best or the worst. Everyone already knew.

The science department occupied a wing of the building that bordered a local neighborhood community. It bordered it to the point that neighbors would often complain about students outside smoking and cutting class in their backyards. Also, a fillable propane station bordered the community. The propane station piped into the science classrooms to their outdated Bunsen burners located on the black lab tables in the upstairs and downstairs classrooms of the wing. It had no real locked gate, but no one ever fooled with the device. No one wanted to start a fire. At least no one wanted to start a fire on purpose.

As students began walking to lunch at 10:20 (a horrible hour to have lunch, but necessary in a large high school) several science teachers closed their doors and began walking to the cafeteria for their part of lunch duty. Mr. Smith stayed behind in his classroom. It was his planning period, and his class would start in half an hour, right after the freshman lunch.

The plan was simple enough. They were discussing the amount of time it takes for certain solids to become liquids, starting with simple ice cubes. He had a tray of ice cubes in the freezer between his lab and the next classroom. He checked the burners were turned off then, as was his routine with ten minutes left, wandered outside to open the valve to turn the gas on before grabbing his coffee from the faculty room and heading back to class.

As his colleague Mr. Smith was making his way to the faculty room for his coffee and two packets of sweetener, Mr. Walsh was sitting in his classroom grading papers. He didn't hear the slight "hiss" coming from the front of the classroom. His desk was toward the back, leaving the front of the class for the large instructor's lab table and the student tables. He never heard the gas leaving the three open ports on two of his lab tables.

Propane is odorless unless odor is added by the delivery company. This has never been a problem, so the school district never asked for an odor to be placed in the gas. After all, their staff were professionals and would be on the lookout for issues whenever the gas system was charged in their classrooms. After five minutes, Mr. Walsh noticed that he began having problems breathing. He thought it was indigestion at first and was confused about what was going on. He hadn't had anything to eat this morning that was different from any other day. His chest began to ache more, and his breathing was more difficult. Slowly the oxygen in his lungs was being replaced by propane; he was being poisoned and he didn't even know it.

Outside the high school, a senior was sneaking out back for a smoke break. He was right under Mr. Walsh's slightly open window, but the old man couldn't hear a thing, the boy reminded himself. He was fine to smoke there. He took out a cigarette and looked around. He still had a few minutes before class.

Mr. Walsh decided that he best see the nurse. He rose quickly, but his legs acted as if he were drunk. He began to lurch forward but stumbled. Outside of the classroom, Mr. Smith was whistling as he made his way back to class. Outside the senior pulled the lighter out of his pocket. The next few seconds would spell the difference between a small emergency and a real disaster.

Mr. Walsh couldn't make it, and he came crashing down into two lab stools nearly ten feet from the door. The crash echoed through the hallway and the senior froze when he heard it from the window inside Mr. Walsh's room. He forgot all about his smoke when he saw Mr. Walsh crawling on the floor and the door to his room swinging open.

Mr. Smith entered the room and couldn't figure out what had happened. Had his friend had a heart attack? He immediately pushed the button on the wall, and when the secretary called over the intercom, he asked her to send the nurse at once. He began talking to Mr. Walsh but just got limited sounds in response. Then Smith noticed another sound. Was that air leaking?

The teacher looked up and noticed that a few of the jets from the gas line were slightly open. "Oh my God," he thought, "I killed him." The teacher quickly exited the room and pulled the fire alarm located next to the classroom and rushed to close the open nozzles. The nurse and the principal ran down the hallway, both with a renewed sense of urgency after hearing the piercing sounds of the fire alarm. Smith filled them in quickly: he had charged the system, and somehow some of Walsh's gas jets were open. He was sure it was propane poisoning.

The principal and Smith pulled Mr. Walsh outside and waited as the nurse began giving him oxygen. The principal left to ensure an orderly evacuation and to wait for the fire department. Smith ran over to the gas valve he had opened less than a half an hour before and shut the valve, stopping the flow into who knew how many open lines.

After the fire department began transporting Mr. Walsh and using large fans to blow the remaining gas out open windows, the fire chief stood next to the principal and Mr. Smith. They discussed the fact that they were lucky there was no ignition source. The chief kicked his boot toward several cigarette butts on the ground next to the door, not ten feet from the propane tank. Had someone lit one of them, this would have been an explosion and certainly Mr. Walsh would have suffered far more from burns in an explosion. They were all very lucky. And the principal looked around and realized that he had no idea what could have happened or how little he was prepared for a situation like this, for a real emergency.

This is how it always begins. Simple things that we all take for granted as we go through our everyday work lives in schools. No one knows for sure when one of these simple things could combine with other simple things to make a large and very complex emergency.

The information you just read was fictional and did not happen. Situations like this *have* occurred, however, many times over the past few decades and will continue to occur into the future. We cannot always prevent them, but we can prepare to manage them.

Another example took place in a middle school science lab that did not have access to any live gas lines. In this case the teachers used large candles to light tea lights for their students to work with. Normally the teachers would light the large candle before class begins, and the students could jump right in when they arrived.

Like so many other underfunded schools around the country, this school did not have funds for regular large candles so teachers supplied their own. This teacher had taken a new one this morning from her home. She placed it on her counter and pulled out the small gas torch to light it. As soon as she lit the wick she realized that this was not a candle. It hissed. She knew it was a firework. She did not want any of the students to be hurt so she did what any good science teacher thought of, starve the oxygen and you cannot have combustion. She placed a beaker over the candle, and the result did not stop the wick but her efforts saved the school. The blast was contained due to her restricting it. Her hand suffered the most damage as broken glass flew through her hands, but there was no firework discharge.

The paramedics helped her, and she retired on disability. It was a painful experience but a sobering reminder that even the smallest and seemingly safest things that we do every day in a school can have deadly consequences. This story, unfortunately, is true. Another principal that day had to look at the pain in this teacher's face and ask himself if he was prepared for this.

We prepare people for their role as a principal—as the educational leader in a school—but we do not always prepare them for being the *safety and emergency leader* of a school. As demonstrated in these examples, there are always opportunities for disaster to strike and a few minutes can mean the difference between all of the staff and students going home safely and some of them not returning home at all.

In the chapters that follow we will discuss ways to take control of an emergency during those critical first few minutes. Capturing that time and making quick and effective decisions can literally be the difference between life and death. Sizing up a situation is critical and must be done as soon as you are aware that there is a problem. As we move forward in the book, you will begin to piece together the mind-set that will allow you to make a difference and have a positive impact on the outcome of an emergency. That process begins quickly, and the first skill you must acquire is the ability to quickly adapt to your role as the emergency leader of the school. Seconds really do count during an emergency.

THE BREAKDOWN

So what started out as one possible emergency quickly escalated to two. In the first scenario with Mr. Smith and Mr. Walsh, we experienced the gas leak, which was preventable and could have been mitigated if proper planning had occurred. Next as a result of the gas leak, we have a medical emergency involving a teacher who was impacted by the leak. Yes, these are two *different* emergencies, even if they had the same cause.

Why do we think of them as two different emergencies? Because they will require different decisions and different resources to effectively manage each emergency. The gas leak must be resolved using fire department equipment and ventilation as well as the effective evacuation and evaluation of any students in the area. The medical emergency will require medical personnel and the nurse to stabilize and transport the victim.

Just because we start off with one issue does not mean that there will not be more to follow! We will return to this scenario several times as you progress through the text. There were ways to mitigate this emergency and reduce its possible impact if not prevent it completely through effective planning and mitigation strategies. For now, it is important to note that there could be more than one emergency at a time and that this will require different incident management techniques but will still be time sensitive and require immediate action to prevent further impact.

LESSONS LEARNED

- Emergencies occur when several small, seemingly inconsequential issues combine to create a larger hazardous condition.
- Most emergencies escalate quickly from a minor issue to a major incident in just a few minutes.
- It is imperative to quickly respond to an emergency in the early stages as it develops. Seconds count.
- Early and decisive action can make a difference in the successful outcome of an emergency.
- Any emergency incident may involve several smaller emergencies that each requires different management tools and techniques.

Chapter 2

Emergency Management Cycle

CREATING A SAFE LEARNING ENVIRONMENT
FROM START TO FINISH

There are literally hundreds of catch phrases that seem to float around the educational realm about emergency plans. You can sometimes hear words like emergency plans, incident command, emergency management, and emergency preparedness and get confused as to which one really means what. They can be different based on what part of the world you are from and whom you are talking with.

Talk to a fire chief and some phrases have a different meaning than what we normally encounter in schools. The goal here is to give you a balanced view of what each one means and how they can be used to make your school a safe place to learn.

Let's start with the two major focus items in this text: the emergency management cycle and incident command system (ICS). They are two different things, but they work together to create a template for how you and your team can respond to any situation. In this chapter we will discuss the emergency management cycle. This is the overall process of managing the way you keep students safe. It has many different components, but they can be easily summed up into what are called the four phases of emergency management: mitigation, preparedness, response, and recovery.

These phases are continuous, which means at any given time you and your school team are in one of these phases when it comes to being prepared for an emergency. If you don't really have a complete emergency plan and are just thinking about emergencies, then you are automatically in the mitigation phase. You are trying to figure out what you could do to manage an incident in your school, thinking about what has happened in the past and asking questions so that you can think about what could happen. Notice the word "think" in all of those answers? The mitigation phase is where you really think about everything; you don't really do much except put thoughts and concepts on paper.

If you finished doing your thinking and began looking at things like what equipment would you need during an emergency or what things you could do to prevent an incident, then you are in the preparedness phase. That is where you find resources to either prevent an issue or reduce the impact of an issue once it occurs. It is also where you find and install the equipment necessary for the times when you have to actually manage an incident. The word "do" is important to note in this phase. You already finished your planning, and now you need to train people or to purchase things that support the work you did in creating your plan. We spend most of our time in the preparedness phase, getting prepared for an emergency after we already planned to have one!

Next is the phase where incident command comes into play: the response phase. You have planned properly and prepared using your mitigation tools, and now when something bad happens, there is an incident. In this phase you actually must use your plan and the tools you acquired to respond to the problem. During this phase we use the incident command system to organize all of our resources and really try to effectively manage the incident and not let the incident manage us.

Incident command systems (ICS for short) are just different sets of tools used to help you manage your emergency response. As you read on, you will also discover that they have other uses as well! In the chapter that covers ICS, we even explain why it is a great way to plan a field trip or even a wedding.

Lastly after an incident is all wrapped up, your team enters the recovery phase. This is the phase of the cycle where you try to return everything in your school to normal, the way it was before there was an incident. If there was a small fire, your recovery phase may include some clean-up efforts and refilling used fire extinguishers. If your school had the unfortunate experience of the passing of a student, then the recovery phase may include a lot of mental health counseling for your students and staff.

Remember, we called this a cycle, which means it returns right back to the beginning. After your school has recovered from whatever happened, you should break out your mitigation phase hat and discuss if you needed to add or change anything in your plan because of the outcome of your response to whatever happened! You take whatever lessons you learned from the incident and try to make sure you capture them in your plan so that team members in the future will learn from your mistakes and be better prepared.

So what is the big difference between these two concepts? Incident command has a beginning and an ending, while the emergency management cycle never stops. That just about covers it! We are always somewhere in the cycle but are not using the ICS unless there is something to command. Figure 2.1

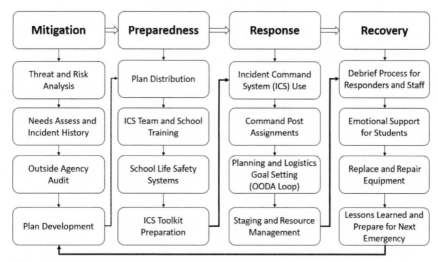

Figure 2.1.   Emergency Management Cycle

shows the relationship between the emergency management cycle and the times we use the ICS. Remember we are always in one of the phases of the cycle but are generally using ICS during the response phase as we are actively managing an incident or an emergency.

EDUCATION FOR EDUCATORS

As educators we are used to dealing with the cycles of student learning from introducing a concept, demonstrating its application to the students, letting them work with the concept, and finally testing to ensure that they understand the concept. Much the same process can be used to understand the emergency management cycle.

We create a lesson plan to go over what we must teach the students, we know we must gather materials and supports to provide them with the hands-on experience during the actual lesson, we give them the lesson using the material we created in the lesson plan and the tools we acquired to let them perform during the lesson, and we test them to see how well they learned the material. After we test them we go back and see how they did and what we could have done to provide better instruction. Well we can really apply those same concepts to preparing for an emergency. Remember there are four phases of emergency management: planning, mitigation, response, and recover.

Let's compare them to our lesson plan example. First, we develop our emergency plan, just like our lesson plan. We need to know what we are preparing for. What could happen (or has already happened) in our school? Once we know what we need to plan for, what tools will we need? If we are teaching a lesson on using an abacus, we need an abacus. If we are planning for an emergency, we need radios, fire extinguishers, lists of students, and things like that. Next we teach the lesson and test the students.

We use our plan to respond to an incident and use the information we created in the lesson plan (mitigation phase) as well as the tools we acquired for the lesson (the preparedness phase) and then we check and see how we did. Simply put the test is this: did everyone go home safe, and did our decisions lessen the impact on the school and student safety (response phase)? Afterward we may need to restock the abacus so that other teachers can use them and see if there is anything that we would change the next time we teach the lesson (recovery phase). There is at least one chapter in the book that goes more in depth into all of these different phases to really allow you to get a better grasp of how they work and how to implement each one!

Like student learning, everything begins with a plan. An emergency plan begins with a planning session. We prepare for the events that are likely and the events that are possible to occur in our school. That is not to say that we're going to be able to plan for every possibility. It is unrealistic to think that we can drill and practice and even document every possible scenario. On September 11, the United States encountered an emergency unlike any it had ever seen. It is clear that we see new and different types of emergencies every day, so we can never really plan for every possible contingency—so don't even try.

In fact, as you begin to really break down the nature of different emergencies, you will see that they are often a combination of different emergencies that all come together at the same time. Our goal in mitigation is to look at likely initial incidents and how we would begin to respond to meet their needs.

This initial phase requires some time and effort and research. It's helpful to contact your local police and fire department to get the history of what actually has occurred in your school. Local media can also be a good source. Also this is the best place to develop your team mentality. Use the skills and historical perspectives from the faculty room.

In every school there is a teacher who has been there since the school bell was installed and remembers when their first students wrote on slate tablets. Talk to them and see what has happened in the school and how it was handled back then. It is good to learn from those lessons so you don't make mistakes, and it gives you the side benefit of showing the staff that you are an inclusive leader who respects their opinions.

It is also important to realize that every person in the school has a role in planning and mitigation efforts. While not every employee of the school may be involved in the emergency response or the ICS, certainly everyone can play a role in looking for issues that may impact the school or that may be dangerous and in trying to help mitigate those dangers.

One of the things that you can do as part of your mitigation cycle is a staff skills assessment to determine which staff members may have a specialized skill set that would assist you in your planning, mitigation, response, or recovery efforts. Personnel who were volunteer firefighters, former law enforcement officers, or even former members of the military may have specialized skills that could really help in the planning efforts as well as help you to respond to emergencies. These staff members usually have some skills and an experience level that allows them to adapt well to stressful situations.

Remember if you are a combat veteran from Afghanistan or Iraq, then a small fire in the cafeteria is not really a huge deal. Utilize those skills if at all possible not only in your planning and your mitigation efforts but more importantly in your response efforts. These people should have a role in your incident command team if it at all possible. Even if they are teachers with responsibility for students, find a staff member who does not have teaching responsibilities and who automatically responds to the classroom to relieve that teacher so that they can assume a role in the ICS team.

You should always remember that an emergency plan is not just a single document that sits up on a shelf and during an issue you break out to discuss how to address a problem. Your team should work together to consistently work on the plan and keep thinking about their roles in keeping kids safe. Again, it is all about the mentality.

An emergency plan is a living document; it should be updated and reviewed regularly to make sure that new information is included. If you add a new way into your school or change the way an old space is configured, these things need to be incorporated in your emergency plan. It should never sit on a shelf, but it should be something that a staff member or better yet several staff members work with regularly. If there's a change such as a stairwell that'll be out of service, someone from the ICS team needs to notify the rest of the staff so that they can address it before a fire drill or worse before a real emergency.

One good habit is to include part of the emergency planning cycle in each of your faculty meetings. Whether this includes discussing changes that you've made that may help mitigate situations that the school encounters or changes that you've made to the response plan to include a different type of emergency situation, the staff members should be briefed so that they are prepared for adapting to those changes. It also reminds the staff that you as a school leader are very much concerned with their safety and safety of the students in your care.

Next look at how to reduce the likelihood of the possible situations that you may encounter based on your mitigation phase work. This involves making sure that you have the right equipment necessary to address the issues that you discovered in your planning. It also includes making some physical changes to your school that may prevent or minimize the impact of some of the issues that you addressed in your mitigation. For instance, you may discover that the shrubs around the school can some times reduce the visibility of threats that may approach the school. In this particular case an act of mitigation includes trimming down those bushes to make the approach to the school more visible.

OK, some of you just stopped reading to look at the packet your chief financial officer gave you that contains your building budget. You are looking at the line items and saying out loud most likely, "I don't have any money for an emergency plan." Well, you don't need any money to plan, and most of the things that you need you already have.

Mitigation is not necessarily about buying new state-of-the-art technology or preparing for events that may never happen, but it's about finding the things that you already have and making sure you can use them during an emergency. It's also about looking at your campus and the attitude of your staff to be better prepared for an emergency. Cost for an attitude change? Zero!

Remember we said that our role as a school is similar to being parents to all of our students? Well, how many of the best parents out there have a well-written plan for responding to an emergency? (And parents who are fire chiefs or police officers don't count here; they may have a written-out plan, but don't hold that against them!) Those parents who don't have a written-out plan do, however, look around them for things that can prevent their kids from getting injured and mentally prepare for an emergency. It's why they make long lists with telephone numbers for the babysitter. That's planning and mitigation! If you have sharp edges on your tables in the living room, you take those tables out when your kids are toddlers so they don't fall and hurt themselves. Cost is nothing, but it reduces the possibility of our kids having an accident and getting hurt. That's mitigation!

We all know that there are some risks that cannot be planned away into obsolescence. There is some risk that is unavoidable. In order to address this, we may find ways to reduce the possible impacts of those risks. It is a method of finding materials or processes which may reduce the possible impact of an issue. For example, if a staff member notices that the walk-off rugs in the front of the school keeps slipping when students come into the school on rainy days, mitigation might include finding a nonslip type of mat that will not slip when kids step on it. That is not planning to do something but actually putting something in place that reduces the possible impact.

We all are aware of what the response phase of the emergency planning cycle is. Most emergency plans are based on how we would respond to an actual emergency. The problem with those emergency plans is they don't include planning what possible situations could occur as well as finding ways to reduce the impact of those situations. By using the entire emergency planning cycle you realize that emergency planning and response become a normal part of the operating culture of your school. The goal is to protect kids as well as educate them and that becomes part of your school culture.

So we will talk about the response to how we assume the different roles of the ICS in a later chapter, but for now know that the responding to an emergency is only part of the overall emergency management cycle and just one of the things that you want to be involved with to become a successful principal whose focus is also on the safety of students.

Once the disaster has been dealt with or averted, you enter the last phase of the cycle, recovery. In recovery, you address issues such as what lessons you learned while you were responding to the incident, what resources you needed but didn't have, and what impact the incident had on your staff and students. Mental health recovery is another huge aspect of recovery. We say that recovery isn't over until the school returns to "normal operations."

The last part is also often overlooked, and that's the recovery phase. In this phase we not only restore the physical school back to its original condition after an incident who we also began to focus on the mental well-being of those impacted by an emergency. For instance, if there were an accidental death of the student, the entire staff and student body will be emotionally impacted by the incident. The recovery phase often involves utilizing mental health professionals and school counseling professionals in a way that helps address the emotional and mental needs of the students and staff after an incident.

We should note here that how long a school takes to return to normalcy depends on the nature of the incident that it has experienced. Reality and history remind us that schools such as Columbine and Sandy Hook that experienced traumatic and deadly incidents we know will never really "return to normal." In fact, we know that those schools will forever experience something that we call the "new normal." It's not that we as people are just comfortable with the fact that that school must experience a new normal, but the reality is students have to return to school and learning must continue.

Even after a tragedy, we must find a way back to normalcy even if it looks or feels different than it did in the past. Whether it is the horrific terrorist strikes of September 11 or the troubling string of violent encounters in schools, as a society we must do what we can to try to continue to live our lives and help our students to live theirs even in the face of such traumas and challenges. We will go over this concept in much greater detail in the recovery chapter (chapter 12), so stay tuned!

Now that all of the planning is finished and we have mitigated what we can, we are prepared for an emergency that we can respond to in the next phase. In the response, we use our resources to respond to anything that is out of the ordinary and meets the requirements of either an emergency or an incident. If it has an impact on students, we can use the ICS to respond to it.

As we will see later, you can also use it to plan for major events such as graduation and field trips. It is a tool like any other that is in your toolbox for you and your staff—whenever you decide you need it. Activate it if you feel that your team would be beneficial. Do not hesitate because the more the ICS team operates together, the better they will be at responding when a real crisis occurs.

So that's it right? When we return to normalcy, it is all over? The cycle just stops? Well, in a word: no! The cycle never stops. You take the information that you learned from this response, and you move right back into the start of the cycle into planning. Now you have more knowledge and can adjust your plan to better meet your needs in the future. The cycle is like a wheel; it keeps on turning and you are *always* in one of the phases of the cycle, whether you know it or not! Most time we spend in the mitigation cycle looking for things to correct, but we are still always in one or the other parts of the cycle.

LESSONS LEARNED

- Emergency management cycle and incident command are two separate entities.
- There are four phases in the emergency management cycle: mitigation, preparedness, response, and recovery.
- Your school is *always* in the middle of one of the four phases of the cycle.
- We use the incident command system (ICS) during the response phase as a way to better organize and manage our efforts to respond during an incident.

Chapter 3

Mitigation Phase of the Cycle

In the beginning there was . . . well . . . nothing. Unlike the big bang, there will not suddenly be a document there for you to use or reference in an emergency if one doesn't already exist. It will just be a blank page. Now all you need is to find the right words to fill the blank page! So, let's start planning what those words will be. That's right; we are entering the mitigation phase. The beginning of the emergency management cycle involves developing a comprehensive plan for how we would address an emergency that we may experience in a school.

That process, like any other, begins with an assessment of what events we have experienced in the past and what events we are likely to experience in the future. This is also the part of the process that will require the most stakeholders. You'll utilize the resources of your local public safety agencies such as police or fire departments, your local emergency management agency as well strategic partners in the insurance community to develop a comprehensive list of issues that you need to address.

All we're doing in this phase is looking at issues such as what are the weather patterns that are common in the area of the school. If the school is located in low-lying areas that are extremely susceptible to flooding, we know that we're going to have to spend time discussing mitigation efforts and how we respond in the event of a flood. If your school is located on top of a mountain, flooding may be less of an issue than a history of wind-driven events.

Where is a good place to start with such a background review? How about starting in your faculty room? Every school has one or two staff members that still remember the school's old slate chalkboards and when it was considered acceptable to paddle students. Talk to those faculty members who have seen the school evolve over many years. See what incidents they recall from their years in the school and how the school handled those incidents.

These staff members will remember quite well experiences and issues from the past. You are looking for fires or whether the school had flooded or been closed due to a tornado. Is your school system susceptible to hurricanes as some of the East Coast schools are? The staff members can tell you very quickly if your school experienced these events.

Next, reach out to your local volunteer or paid fire company. They could look back at what is called your premise history or the history of your property. This will tell you what emergencies in the past five to ten years the fire department has responded to at your school. Certainly there will be a lot of medical emergencies involving staff members and students but you're also looking for events such as fires or other hazardous material incidents or situations that were out of the ordinary.

This premise history will let you know not only what emergency incidents occurred in a school but also will give you an idea of how often they occur. Part of your planning process is prioritizing these incidents that occur the most often. Figure 3.1 helps you manage the relevance of different events. This is called the priority quad, and it is a great planning tool.

Along the left side we see two different sections: low frequency and high frequency. Just as the names suggest, low-frequency events do not occur very

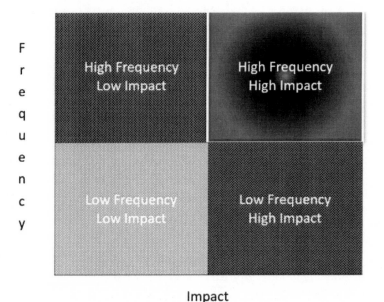

Figure 3.1.   Risk Assessment Priority Grid

often while high-frequency events are more regular like medical emergencies or, in a high school, fights between students.

At the bottom we see the two sections: low impact and high impact. Low-impact events do not impact or threaten to impact a large number of students or have a reduced threat of physical damage. If you have minor medical issues, these are usually high frequency; low-impact incidents are normally not life-threatening and impact only one or a few students. A high-impact event would be an incident such as an active shooter threat, which threatens a large number of students but also could result in catastrophic loss of life. Thankfully these are considered low-frequency, high-impact events.

So where do you focus your planning efforts? You begin by looking at the high-frequency events and focus on all of them. Your top priority would be high-frequency, high-impact events. Hopefully you do not have very many events in that category. Most schools thankfully do not. Next we focus on high-frequency, low-impact events, which is usually the biggest line on the graph.

Next we focus on low-frequency, high-impact events. These incidents are rare but have the potential for a large loss of life or significant impact so they require our planning efforts. Just a little time on this quadrant could go a long way in the terrible event that an incident of this nature occurs. Remember, we do not ever say that something cannot happen at our school. Time and history has shown us that anything can happen anywhere.

REACH OUT TO YOUR LOCAL FIRST RESPONDERS

Next you do a similar graph with your local police department. If your school has experienced multiple issues involving parental custody disputes, that may be something you want to address first. The police can tell you how often they've been called up with such complaints. And this can also help you in your mitigation efforts if they've responded to your school for issues such as vandalism multiple times over the recent years.

Your state or county emergency management agency is also a key partner in developing the risk assessment for your school. They can tell you about the natural disasters that have been experienced in your community dating back several decades. You may find out that while your school has experienced many emergencies, several times the school has operated as an emergency shelter for other communities that are flood prone during the past several decades. Again while this is not an emergency, it is something you would incorporate as part of your school emergency plan. Even though you are not opening your school up for students to learn, you still need a plan for how you and your staff open the school as an emergency shelter during a natural disaster.

Usually emergency management agencies (EMAs) also are very adept at utilizing the emergency management cycle. Use their knowledge and their skills to help you in your process of developing your new plan. They can not only help you look at what emergencies and incidents you should incorporate in your plan, but also how to communicate that process as you develop your plan. They can help you develop a structure for your emergency plan that will make it easy to use and easy for your staff to incorporate in their daily routine.

Some states have an office of school safety as part of one of their state agencies. Usually the Department of Education or the state Department of Public Safety has an office that is specifically designed to address the needs of schools as they plan for different emergencies. Take advantage of these professionals who have worked with your colleagues in other schools, and use their knowledge to assist you in your planning process.

It's not cutting corners when you utilize someone else's material if you know that that materials have been tested and work. In fact, emergency planning is one of those areas where it is exceptionally important not to reinvent the wheel. We focus on best practices because if they work in one school, it is likely that some of those practices will work well in your school. There's no greater compliment than imitating another successful program!

USE THE WORLD WIDE WEB

There are also many school safety–related websites that include risk analyses that are provided by insurance carriers. The federal government's Federal Emergency Management Agency and the U.S. Department of Education both have excellent resources to help schools in the initial design phase of their emergency plan. Again most of these resources are free to schools all throughout the country. No one wants to be accused of making a profit in order to make children safe! That is why most federal and state programs provide free assistance to schools that are creating an emergency plan.

WE KNOW WHAT HAPPENED, NOW DO WE HAVE ANY TOOLS?

Now you have a good basic list of some of the emergencies that your school has encountered, and you have prioritized those threats. Next you will want to look at what resources you have at your disposal to respond to those threats. Whether those are your staff members or physical equipment such as fire extinguishers or a sprinkler system, you need to know what is available and what you can incorporate in your response plan. This is also where your staff skills inventory may come into play as you develop the structure of your ICS team.

One thing that we should address here is setting realistic priorities as you develop your incident response plan. The fire department and police department may have very complicated emergency response plans for your school. They have very difficult and complex roles during incidents involving schools. However, our role in the school emergency has two primary missions and only two. Our goal as we develop our incident response plan is to find ways to *maintain accountability for every student and ensuring their continued safety*. In other words, our sole mission is to know where the kids are and that they are safe. That's it. So as you're developing your plan remember that our mission is simple, *know where the kids are and that they are safe.*

As you develop your plan, you should look at situations to determine how your school has responded in the past and incorporate that as well as best practices in your decision making. For instance, a few staff members at a school explained how there was a boiler room fire fifteen years ago and one of the evacuation sites put students close to the area that firefighters were accessing to fight that fire. After learning that information, you may want to change your evacuation sites so that the same issue does not occur again. You can also look at sample emergency plans that are on the web to find ways that other school districts address the same issues in their plans.

As we focus on each situation and how we would respond to it, remember that some of the people in your plan may change from time to time so you should not use specific names in your planning. If your principal's name is "Howard," then in the management cycle, utilize the name "principal" rather than "Howard." You want to focus on the *role* that people play, not the individuals who assume that role. In this way if one of your key staff members is absent, his or her replacement will be able to focus on what is required of that role and not on that individual. It is also important to make sure that as you are training members in the emergency plan, you don't only train those specific individuals to respond, but also an alternate person for each important role in your team. You should incorporate training of your ICS team as an important part of your emergency plan.

There are many ways of incorporating different response strategies in a document such as an emergency response plan. In some cases, some schools like to include what each member of the school team would be thinking about or managing during an event. They even include expectations for classroom teacher, members of the emergency team, and other support members of the staff. In other cases, the emergency plan is written based on the ICS and simply describes what roles each member of the team will assume during this particular event. Really those decisions are entirely up to you and your team.

If you have a relatively small school and will have a limited emergency response team, you may want a focus on a plan that can be incorporated readily by the entire staff since they will have to support you in managing any major event. If you are with a large school, you may want focus on a more "ICS team"-related plan that will develop a foundation of knowledge for your ICS team who will then support members of your general school community in the response.

Looking at the likelihood that an incident will occur and the size of the possible impact will provide some clues as to how many resources you should build around an issue. Resources management is an area where your plan must be careful and *conservative*. You cannot incorporate resources from other agencies in your plan. It is easy to assume that under your plan you can note that "the fire department will extinguish the fire," but you don't know if the fire department will be available to help you when the fire occurs. The purpose of an *internal* emergency plan is to help you utilize *internal* resources to help manage an incident.

The agencies that respond to assist you from the fire service or the police departments all have their own emergency plan, and it does not incorporate your personnel. They are prepared to assume their role as soon as they arrive just as you should prepare your staff to assume their roles prior to the fire department or the police department arrives. You can manage an incident only with what you have available, so do not count on or plan for anything beyond your resources. Also, do not focus on performing tasks that are beyond the scope of what you are supposed to accomplish. In case we haven't said it enough, your first and most important tasks are to know where all the students are and to keep them safe!

It is also imperative that you're honest in your assessment of your facilities' ability to respond to an emergency. Do not document resources in your plan that you do not have available. For example, if you do not have a flashlight for every classroom in the event of a power failure, do not incorporate a flashlight in every classroom as part of your plan. If you are able to get funding for flashlight after you have developed your plan, you can easily change the plan to incorporate utilizing a flashlight in each classroom. Assume as you develop your plan that it is effective for the day that you created it, not based on things that you assume are going to happen. Prepare your staff today for what they can respond to today.

There are also several trains of thought as far as whether you address every situation in a checklist-style manner or whether you create a role-driven emergency plan. Normally emergencies do not fit into a pre-made, predetermined checklist. There is always something different or something that has changed that won't be incorporated into a checklist. (Unfortunately, most emergencies do not take the time to read your plan before they occur.) Too many times emergency responders in the school community become very focused on checklists rather than being very focused on their role in an emergency. Sometimes the narrow focus of checklists can create tunnel vision in your staff. It is imperative that we remain focused on the totality of the circumstances rather than the specifics of a checklist.

In the response section of the book, we discuss assuming roles such as incident commander, planning section chief, and logistics section chief. In your plan you may want to create brief statements on what each of these staff members should be considering as they assume that role during a different type of emergency. These tips are often called "job aides" and help them to think as they assume their roles but do not force them to use an "inside-the-checklist" mentality.

Your plan should also include sections on training your staff and who is responsible for training individual staff members in their role as an emergency responder. You should include a section regarding drills and exercises in which you plan your monthly fire drill as well as at least three annual lockdown drills. We will discuss tabletop exercises later in the book. These are great tools for your team. You sit down as a team and talk your way through how you would respond to a different type of emergency. It is a great way to think as a group and gets you to gel more effectively. Your incident command staff should have at least one tabletop exercise per year. This will allow your staff to prepare for their roles that they will assume during an actual emergency. The members of your local emergency management agency are experts at how you conduct a tabletop exercise and most are more than willing to assist you as you develop the tabletop exercise plan for your school. They may even be willing to come in and act as the moderator for just such an exercise.

Your emergency plan should also include things that are necessary to assist outside agencies in how they respond to your school. It should include an appendix that has floor plans for the school as well as the location of important facility structures such as the gas shutoff or power shutoff for the school. If your school is equipped with electronic access control, the areas of your school that can be accessed with a key card should be highlighted on one of your floor plans. *It is important that the floor plan you provide in your emergency plan is current.* If your school has changed room numbers or has been reconfigured by your facilities department recently, change the way your floor plan appears in your appendix to your emergency plan.

In this way you can provide responding fire agencies with a floor plan of your school that will be accurate and lets them know where those key features are around the school that they need to access during an emergency. In the event of a hostile person in the school where seconds can mean the difference between life or death for a student or staff member, being able to tell the police quickly and correctly where the threat is located inside the school is imperative. If the floor plan that you provided to police has different numbers than what police officers will encounter in the hallway, it creates a hazard to both you and the police officers.

LESSONS LEARNED

- Begin by looking at what impacts and hazards exist in your community.
- Your mitigation process includes looking at what natural and man-made disasters have occurred in your area.
- There are resources in your state and local governments such as the fire and police departments that can help look at potential issues based on historical information.
- Be honest when you look at what your school is equipped to handle and what it is not prepared to address.
- Emergency plans are not about checklists. They are about people being trained to adapt to each incident or emergency.
- Work with your local police and fire department closely because they are truly your first line of defense and your first helping hands during an emergency. The more they know, the safer your school and the people inside it are!
- Remember the main objective for you and your school ICS team is always to know where the students are and to keep them safe.

Section II

PREPAREDNESS

Chapter 4

Preparedness Phase

CAN'T PREVENT IT, BUT WE CAN MAKE IT HURT LESS!

Preparedness is the phase of the emergency cycle that you will spend the most time operating under. You have your plan in place, and you have trained for the "big event," but nothing has happened yet. So now all you can do is sit and wait (as well as the other stuff you get paid to do, like make sure the teachers teach and that the students learn!)

Preparedness is when you try to take your plan and look at ways to reduce the impact of certain emergencies or ways to reduce the risk of something occurring in your school. We all know that you cannot possibly eliminate all the risk of operating a school, but you can do things to make them less likely or have less of an impact.

Preparedness is not always about spending money to buy new tools to help you respond to an incident or rebuilding parts of the school so there is no possible way someone can get hurt. These are costly, and often it is difficult to justify spending money to avoid having an issue that may not have ever occurred in the past. Sometimes it is about making sure you have the tools necessary to help if that area becomes an issue.

For example, when we started ensuring that students with disabilities had open access to every aspect of any other child's education, we knew that there might be a challenge in getting all students out of the building in a timely fashion if we could not use elevators during a fire. Some preparedness strategies that address this include spending money on an evacuation stair device designed to help quickly deliver a wheelchair downstairs.

Another cheaper form of preparedness for the same situation may be ensuring that two or three staff members are assigned to physically remove the student using a smaller portable stair chair and carrying the lighter stair chair down the stairs during a real emergency. Using people power can help reduce the cost of mitigation; you just have to make sure that they know what you want them to do! This also eliminates worry about the equipment failing when there is an actual emergency.

Keeping an eye out for obvious risks is another important part of the preparedness mentality. If it is raining when the students come in and you know that the floors are slippery when wet, post a sign there or add several walk-off mats to reduce the chance that they will fall. Maybe even ask a staff member to stand there as students come in and remind them that the floors may be slippery.

A preparedness strategy does not only apply to preventing an incident or reducing possible impacts, but also involves getting tools to help you better manage an incident when it occurs. For instance, purchasing an automatic external defibrillator (or seeking donations or a grant to buy one) and training the staff to use it is a form of preparedness. It does not prevent someone from going into cardiac arrest, but it does add a tool that can hopefully reduce the impact and offer a better chance for survival to the victim.

KEEPING UP WITH CHANGE THROUGH PREPAREDNESS

Schools are ever-changing entities, and rooms change their uses on an almost annual basis. Sometimes it is hard to keep up with those changes. Part of your preparedness process should include making sure you revisit all of the classrooms and spaces in your school that change their use or are altered by a renovation or repair.

Have the uses for the room changed? Remember in the mitigation phase we reviewed why it is important to make sure that room numbers on floor plans provided to public safety agencies are accurate? That occurs during this phase as well. If your district takes down a wall and creates one large classroom out of two smaller ones, make sure you change the plan to include the new configuration and number on the floor plans.

Did you add a new computer lab? Does a new computer lab offer any different risks than a regular classroom? These rooms usually have significant wiring added to be able to supply a large number of computers. Those computers also usually are hot when operating. All of these things should be considered. Perhaps there was a fire extinguisher in the classroom closet but it was an old water can-type fire extinguisher. Will that work on an electrical fire? (Hopefully all of our readers are thinking back quickly to remember that water conducts electricity and the new computer lab has lots of electricity!)

So preparedness may include replacing the water fire extinguisher with a CO_2 extinguisher that will work on electrical fires. What about asking the district electrician to install an in-classroom kill switch to cut off the power to all the computers at once if there is a problem? Then the teacher doesn't have to wait for a breaker that might not trip off during an electrical problem, but they would have the ability to turn off the power themselves.

UNLOCKING THE SECRETS TO LOCKING THE DOORS

Ever since the term "lockdown" came into our vocabulary, there has been debate after debate about the easiest and fastest way to lock classroom doors. Some experts will show you that installing simple push buttons on the inside of the door is the easiest and fastest way. Then ask a middle-school teacher who will explain that those rambunctious kids will lock you out of your own classroom.

What about doors where there is a key lock on the inside *and* the outside? As an experiment, go into one of your classrooms and with a sense of urgency ask the teacher there to lock the door. Next, start counting the seconds and watch the teacher. Some may have the key right around their neck, but many will have it on their desk, in their desk drawer, or in a purse or knapsack. They will begin to fumble around. Seconds will tick away and if you asked them with a sense of urgency, they will start to breathe a little bit heavier and they will begin to lose a bit of their fine motor skills. Once they get the key, watch their hands and head as they try to guide the key into the keyway. Their hands may shake and their hand-eye coordination is slightly diminished because of the jump in their adrenaline and their body's response to the perceived threat.

There is nothing wrong with their response. In fact, we can anticipate it because we know how the human body handles stress. Remember that this is not even a real emergency. There are no alarms sounding or odd smells and noise that would indicate an emergency. It is just you "creating" a perceived threat by using a sense of urgency in your voice. They don't have a choice but to respond that way. Their senses are just naturally fearful based on your directions.

One of the things we can do to help is to find ways to reduce the amount of thought and physical activity needed to accomplish lifesaving tasks. One simple fix is to take a small magnetic strip and place it over the hole in the door strike that receives the locked part of the door. Now, if the teachers lock their door, the door will still be able to open and close without locking. If there is a call for a lockdown, the teacher can crack the door slightly and simply push the strip out of the way and pull the door closed. (Total cost is about ten cents.)

PLAYGROUNDS: A PREPAREDNESS NIGHTMARE

When you walk outside an elementary school, you stumble across the school nurse's evil nemesis: the joyful land of happily playing children as well as broken arms, legs, hands, and a thousand lost teeth! Yes, we all know that kids get hurt on the playground. We also know that it is absolutely impossible to get rid of the playground. (Who would want to? Just picture a classroom full of first-graders who have not been allowed to play after six hours. That spells "mutiny!")

So what can we do to keep playgrounds safe? First, look down at what's under them. Is there enough play mulch to allow children to fall without getting injured from your higher play devices? What kind of mulch is it? In some cases, the new molded rubberized material is great for shock absorption. Is it located around all of the play devices where a student can fall? Has it been inspected to ensure that the material is still intact, and that there are no tears or separated edges?

How about monitoring? Are there enough monitors around to keep an eye on how the students are playing? Every day at Walt Disney World there are literally hundreds of employees monitoring rides that are designed to be safe cocoons for the occupants. We all have playground equipment that is far more dangerous than any ride at Disney with no one monitoring how the kids use it.

Sometimes this can be a re-training effort for preparedness. Spend a little time outside at an elementary school recess, and you will usually find the teachers huddled up and talking together. This means you have a lot of resources that cannot all monitor every different aspect of the play yard from one location. Assign them locations so that you spread them out. Assign them closer to activities that are dangerous or that have a history of accidents.

Another great trend is creating a "walking trail" around your playground for the staff. Measure it and encourage staff to wear their sneakers and not walk together but walk around the play area. They will enjoy the exercise as much as the students do, and they will be a moving set of eyes rather than a stationary set!

Also, *be age restrictive.* There are some activities that are designed for older students. Make sure teachers enforce those rules. Keep the little ones off those devices, and at the same time make sure the big kids don't hog the devices designed for the little ones. That will keep all the kids happy and still keep your students safe at the same time. This will also reduce your legal liability. If the manufacturer says for students eight and up and you allow a seven-year-old to use the device, you are incurring liability for knowingly not using the equipment as instructed.

USING DRILLS TO HELP IN THE PREPAREDNESS PROCESS

Every time that you have a lockdown drill or a fire drill, there is a chance for you to learn something that can be applied to preparedness. In one school its fire drills went well, but the classes who were evacuated furthest from the school could never hear the directions to come back in. The solution didn't cost anything because they figured out that they could use a device that was already hanging around the gym teacher's neck. You guessed it—a whistle. When the all-clear signal came, they made sure the gym teacher blew his whistle three times quickly (and loudly) letting everyone in the back of the school know it was all clear.

Post an employee at each exit door for one of your drills and see how long it takes before all of the classes who use that exit manage to clear the school. Is there one exit that takes a minute or so longer than another exit near it? Perhaps switching one class to the other exit will decrease the lag time at the first exit and get kids out on average faster?

Use the fire department to help during these drills as well. They may point out to you that several of your classes exit right past where the fire apparatus will access the school or near the fire hydrant that they use. They may recommend to you to correct that issue by choosing another location for those classes to assemble to free the area where the trucks come in.

Also remember to try different pull stations for your alarms! Let different adults pull the stations at different locations to make sure that you don't have a failure in your system somewhere. Change things up just to keep yourself and your team fresh. The emergencies that you encounter are never predictable so you should not be either!

LOOKING FOR A SIGN?

Another great and inexpensive preparedness tool may be adding different signs around the school that will help during an emergency. Remember that during an emergency, some of the normal things that we think of when we are not under stress become difficult to remember in a crisis. You may have gone to a certain room a hundred times, but when there is a crisis and someone tells you a room number, it may take a minute to gather your thoughts and remember just how to get to that room. Save yourself those costly seconds of recall and label the hallway intersections clearly.

We have all gotten off the elevator in a hotel after checking in, and there are always nice signs right as you get out of the elevator. Room numbers with an arrow pointing to them and even convenient signs for the ice machine and stairs. If it is good enough for a hotel, why not do the same thing for a school? In the event of an emergency, fire crews who may not be familiar with your school could use those signs to help guide them to their destination without needing assistance from your staff.

Are your science rooms labeled as science rooms? Do first responders have to enter the room to see the chemical storage unit or the air hood before they notice that this room has hazardous materials in it? This is a great place for a label on the doors. Just because you label the science wing doesn't mean a gentle reminder at each door would not be a good idea. Every little bit helps in an emergency.

Your school should also have a binder somewhere in the front office or at the command post (we will discuss this important area in the response phase when we talk about incident command) that contains chemical data sheets called material safety data sheets (or MSDS Sheets) that come with every chemical and industrial product that is sold to your school and district. By law these sheets should be kept someplace where they are readily available to first responders.

Because you don't look at these sheets every day, you may not remember the last time you saw the folder. A handy sign in the office window or on your emergency floor plan may be a great reminder of where the MSDS notebook is located during an incident. Better yet, scan each new sheet that comes into your school and in addition to the hard copy book, you can have it on a note-book computer with you as part of your ICS team.

Have you ever walked outside of your school and looked in through the classroom windows? Can you tell from outside quickly which classroom you are looking into? Usually it's pretty hard to look outside and compare what you see outside with what you know things look like from the inside.

Imagine the view from police officers who are outside trying to find a threat or firefighters looking to make access to a certain room from outside. Is there an easy way to label them outside so that first responders can look at the window and see the classroom number that they would recognize from their floor plan? Something small like an index card–sized sign with the number printed on it taped or stuck to the outside window nearest the wall will eliminate this issue and save seconds or even minutes during an emergency.

USE THE KISS PRINCIPLE FOR YOUR EMERGENCY PLANS

Remember the adage "Keep it simple, stupid" (KISS)? Well that absolutely applies to emergency planning. There are hundreds of systems and devices out there designed to make you an excellent ICS team. Some are great tools, but others require more effort than they are worth and tend to complicate the response rather than make it better.

When you review a new process or product for your ICS team, ask yourself simply if the new process or product would make kids safer or not. That is, after all, the overall goal. If it makes it easier for you to manage your incident, then it may be worth giving it a shot.

So a vendor brings you a new app for your iPhone that contains all of the incident command forms and allows you to fill them out and distribute them to your ICS team members with the click of the send key. Sounds like an easy way to organize, right? Begin asking yourself some questions. What if I forgot my phone? What if my battery is dying and I have to stop writing my response plan when it dies? What if any of the members of the team don't have their phones or they don't hear them ring when I send the item? If you have big fingers like some of us, you may find it difficult to type into a form on your phone.

Your graphic arts teacher has a large printer that you can use to print the organization chart and the rough incident action plan. You get a piece of clear plastic and mount the posters to the plastic. Now with a dry erase marker you have a large easy-to-use and change ICS chart that allows you and everyone to see what you decided and what they should be doing. And the plastic will never need to get plugged in and recharged. Problem solved!

LESSONS LEARNED

- Not all preparedness and prevention efforts require a financial investment. Sometimes it is a matter of changing a procedure.
- We cannot eliminate all of the risk in schools, but we can reduce the level of risk and reduce the impact.
- Another form of preparedness includes looking into tools such as automatic external defibrillators, which help reduce the impact of an incident once it occurs.
- Preparedness and prevention tools should make your life easier, not add difficulty. If a procedure or product complicates the process, don't use it.
- Always use tools and procedures that are as easy to do under stress as possible. Remember that the body and mind operate differently under stressful conditions so keep that in mind when planning for operating under stress.
- Think about what can go wrong with equipment that you may want to use during an incident. If there are too many downsides, you may just want to skip using it!
- Take advantage of your drills as an opportunity to test your systems and your team. Emergencies are not predictable so neither should your response plans.

Section III

RESPONSE

Chapter 5

Response Phase and Incident Command

Now that you have a decent grasp of the emergency cycle, let's begin getting a grasp on what incident command is and how we can master the skills necessary to protect our staff and students. First, let's look at the history of incident command and what the benefits are.

When we get to the response part of the emergency management cycle, we begin looking at using a system to organize our response. We have all used some form of the organizer in the past. The ICS is an organizer for incident command. It is a way to keep in mind the important things that need to be managed and how they can readily be addressed.

WHAT EXACTLY IS AN INCIDENT COMMAND SYSTEM?

So what is ICS? It dates back to the 1970s and wildland firefighters on the West Coast. Every year out-of-control forest fires would require thousands of firefighters from agencies all over the country, if not the continent, to work together to extinguish. The problem that forest firefighting leaders discovered is that these trained professionals also spoke different languages, used different codes on the radio, and had different ways to command and control resources they were using in firefighting. How do you quickly and efficiently find a way to ensure that everyone at a single large fire is able to communicate effectively and operate as an integral part of a major firefighting force?

Each time there was a conflagration, it took time to bring in resources, train their personnel, and make sure that they would be effective at the fire. Time is a luxury that we do not have at a major emergency. In response, the people who managed these fires, the U.S. Forest Service, began creating a system that would allow all of these groups to work together seamlessly. It just had a few requirements:

1. It had to be expandable to meet the needs of different types and sizes of events.
2. It had to use common terminology so that each first responder could understand the instructions and communications without delay or interpretation.
3. Limited span of control, often too many workers or firefighters were asked to work for too few command officers. That meant it was hard to delegate effectively as well as to manage accountability and safety for those you were responsible for.
4. Universal structure, which would address the same primary areas of need for managing any incident: *operations, planning, logistics,* and *finance.*

Once all of these things had been addressed in one comprehensive system, they could be applied to nearly any emergency that would be handled by any emergency response agency in the world. The glory of the new system is that it also crosses boundaries between emergency response organizations and other public service agencies, such as utility companies, public works, and yes, even education. Once everyone becomes trained in the system, they can be used by all of the agencies that are required to manage difficult emergencies. Everyone speaks the same language and understands the incident command process as well as all of the titles and jobs used in the ICS.

WHY INCIDENT COMMAND WORKS IN SCHOOLS

When we look at the ICS and its benefit in schools, there are a few factors to keep in mind. First, this new system tries to take us away from the checklist emergency management mentality that we all had in schools for most of the decades that we have all had school emergency plans. Over the years there have been flip charts and there have been slick-laminated binders with tabs representing different types of emergencies.

There is one problem with having a checklist mentality: what if something happens that needs to be addressed, but is not on the checklist? Will someone remember to do it? What if the emergency doesn't fit in with any of the scenarios that were planned for when the checklists were developed? One last problem with the checklist is everyone has to have it and understand how it works and most emergencies that we face will not have had time to read the checklist so they will do whatever they can to deviate from your plan! (That is right, we said the "emergency" will not read your plan, and some of your staff may not as well!)

So we need a system that teaches us to assume roles and responsibilities regardless of the nature of the incident. Each member of the ICS team is trained in a particular area of the system and will assume their job function no matter what they are faced with. As we look at the different roles in the next section, think about your high school drama club. Each year your drama teacher is the director, no matter what the type of play. We all remember how some kids were just always going to be the lead actors. They lived for acting in their high school plays. So if the fall play was a comedy, they played the lead. If it was a drama, they played the lead.

This is how we need to think about these roles in the ICS. No matter what type of an incident, your team will assume those roles and focus on what each is supposed to do. Now when you call for the ICS team, you do not need to assign someone to a specific task; they already know their jobs and like a well-trained and well-oiled machine, they do their jobs without having to be prompted.

MEET THE CAST OF YOUR ICS TEAM

Now that you know the history of incident command, let's continue to think about your incident like a play and look at your cast! First, every play needs a director and that would be your *incident commander*. Normally this is the principal. This is the person in charge. All the decisions go through the incident commander. The incident commander has to be accessible and have communications with everyone involved. The commander needs to be aware of the situation and works with the supporting cast to develop and implement a plan of action.

The lead actor is the *operations section chief*. This is the person on stage that does all the work in front of everyone. If there is something that

Incident Commander	
Responsibilities:	Characteristics:
• Person in charge of the incident. • Approve goals for the incident. • Ensure that the operation focuses on accountability and safety of students and staff. • Request additional resources as necessary to achieve the goals of the operation.	• Ability to focus on the overall situation and think strategically. • Ability to communicate effectively. • Ability to delegate effectively. • Ability to manage the strategic goals of the operation. • Ability to work well with the rest of their ICS team to manage the incident.

Figure 5.1.   Incident Commander Job Description

physically has to be done, the operations section (which the operations section chief leads) will handle it. They do any physical task that is required. In figure 5.2 you can see the list of responsibilities that your operations team may need to accomplish.

For instance, during a bomb scare, these people would be the ones who physically work with the police to search the school. In an evacuation, they are the staff members who take the roles and ensure student accountability as well as provide the interior search to ensure that everyone is out of the school. Usually this branch is run by your school facility operations personnel, custodians, or maintenance technicians. They have a working knowledge of where everything is in the school and generally have the best access.

Next in your supporting cast is the *planning section chief*. This is the person who will look at the situation and the totality of the circumstances to begin thinking of what possible plans and actions should come next. For instance, in a bomb threat, they are less concerned about how the evacuation of students is going, they are thinking about the "what's next" for the incident. If it is cold outside, they are already thinking about getting buses for heat and possibly to move students to another location.

These folks try to stay one step ahead of the incident. Usually an experienced administrator is great in this role. They know how schools work and can really begin to look at what is needed to keep the students safe and what they should recommend to the incident commander for next steps. They look for reasonable alternatives and then begin making a plan for what would the most prudent and reasonable next step be.

Operations Section Chief	
Responsibilities:	Characteristics:
• Is responsible for physically implementing the goals of the operation. • Directs all of the physical activities that resources and personnel perform in addressing the goals of the operation. • Ensures the safety of all of the resources and staff performing various tasks at the incident scene. • Determines what tasks are required to accomplish the goals of the operation and assign personnel to achieve those tasks.	• Ability to communicate effectively. • Ability to prioritize tasks based on the situation and needs of the operation. • Ability to recognize and address safety issues that they notice during the operation. • Ability to organize and to maintain accountability of all of the resources and staff member operating at the scene.

Figure 5.2.   Operations Section Chief Job Description

Planning Section Chief	
Responsibilities:	Characteristics:
• Is responsible for looking at the current status of the incident and recommending goals that could be implemented in order to manage the incident. • Ensures that any recommended plan addresses the two primary concerns for the command staff, knowing where all students are and that they are safe. • Works with logistics section chief to find what resources are needed to accomplish the recommended goals.	• Ability to communicate effectively. • Ability to think strategically. • Ability to look at the nature of the incident, as well as the outside factors that have an impact on the incident (weather, time of day, etc.) to determine the most effective course of action. • Must be experienced enough to understand the nature of school operations and be aware of the limitations of the students and staff when considering different goals.

Figure 5.3. Planning Section Chief Job Description

They would work with the last key command team member; the stage manager or *logistics section chief* has to sit next to the planning chief and help figure out what they need in order to accomplish the next steps in the plan. The logistics section chief is a sort of a sounding board for possible ideas with the planning chief. If the planning chief says, "hey, let's rent a helicopter to take the students across the street." The logistics chief would look at the planning chief as if they were out of their mind and say, "no, we cannot get a helicopter."

However, if the planning chief says, "hey, let's get buses to take the students down the street to the high school where the auditorium would fit all of the students," then the logistics chief has a real plan that could work and has to figure out what would be required to accomplish that plan. How many buses would be needed to make this happen? If the two quickly determine that there are not enough buses to support their possible plan, they both go back to the drawing board to find the next best alternative.

These are the reasons why your planning and logistics chiefs must work well together and be able to help each other with the plan. Once the plan gets approved, the planning chief can help the logistics chief actually get those resources and get them located where the operations team can use them.

No good play goes on without a good press agent. That's your **district public information officer** (PIO). Communications are going to be a *huge* part of anything that goes on in a school. One of the first resources that you need to get from your district office is your PIO. This person can help your incident commander (let's call them the IC for short, that's what the fire

Logistics Section Chief	
Responsibilities:	Characteristics:
• Works with the planning section chief to determine what resources and staff may be needed to implement the plans and operations recommended to the incident commander. • Appoints a staging area manager to manage the off-site staging area and communicates with the manager to have resources sent to the scene from staging. • Manages the ancillary systems, such as communications, that are needed to manage the incident.	• Ability to communicate effectively. • Ability to think strategically. • Ability to track multiple resources and personnel that are operating either on the scene of the incident or are waiting for assignment in the staging area. • Should be very creative and have the ability to think about alternative resources that may be needed in order to implement the goals of the operation. • Must have access to different communications systems in order to request different resources.

Figure 5.4. Logistics Section Chief Job Description

department will call theirs so now you will have one too!) in determining when and what needs to go out to parents as well as the media.

Usually the PIO will work with other agencies' PIOs (such as the police or fire department spokesperson) and may even have to find a place to create a "joint information center" or JIC. In cases of major events, it is important that the media (and your parents) receive the correct information. If the spokespeople are giving different messages to different media outlets, it could cause confusion. Try to find a way and a place for these communications professionals to work together with the media that will not directly impact the way you and the other agencies are working to actually address the emergency.

LET'S SET THE STAGE: LOOK AT ICS FACILITIES

Now you need to think about where incidents happen in your performance. The stage is, of course, the entire school since this is where the incident is occurring. We call this the incident scene. You need a location to command the incident, just like the control booth in the auditorium, where the ICS team meets and performs their tasks. It is called the **command post.** You should have some way of designating where this location is and how people can readily find it. You do not want people just walking around your scene; they should be able to locate you.

Make it the same spot for every incident if possible. It should be in the front of the school so that when police, fire, and ambulance personnel show up, they know where to report. If possible, have a flag that you can put on a car or even buy a small flashing magnetic green light with a car plug. The flashing green light is universal for command post, and the fire folks will walk right over to you. Just remember to locate it out of the way of first responders. Make sure you do not place it between the fire lane and your school. Then when fire equipment arrives, you will be in the way of hoses or equipment that firefighters may need inside the building. You also want to be far enough away not to be in any danger from the emergency itself!

Now some new administrators are thinking themselves, perhaps even out loud, "but if the emergency doesn't require the school to be evacuated, should we still go outside to the command post?" The answer is no; you can have an inside command post that doesn't have any flashing lights and so on. People from other agencies can just walk in and be directed to your internal command post. No problem at all.

Your command post should have the ICS forms such as copies of the ICS 201 or incident briefing forms. These will help you create your organization chart as well as your incident plan. You will need clipboards and notebooks to jot down notes as you develop possible plans. You should also think about weather. If it is raining, notebooks don't do well outside. Some schools get a small tent that can be quickly set up. A more practical solution can be the use of the back of staff member's SUV. You can use the floor space for papers and other items and discuss plans under the open lift gate.

The next important facility is your backstage, where all the resources and personnel are lined up and ready to go on stage to get to work. We call this area the "**staging area**," and it will be a very important place as more and more folks come to help. This is where all the fire trucks, ambulances, and police cars can park where they will not get in the way until they are needed. It is where your buses will go until you need them to actually drive up to pick up students. If you have a pretty open parking lot or loop access road, this space may be right there on your property. If not, you may talk to the police about letting them stage on the side of the main road outside of your school property so that they don't interfere with anything that is going on at the scene.

It may also be a larger lot close to the school but off the property. You may need to send someone from logistics to the staging area to direct equipment that is needed into the scene. If you have a small lot and the fire department has a lot of apparatus (read fire trucks) on the grounds, you may not be able to line a large number of buses up for your evacuation. You may need to send them one at a time. In that case your operations team is loading and taking accountability of each bus at the scene and when they release a bus, they call logistics at the staging area to send in the next bus. In a later chapter we will go more into detail about the benefits of a well-managed staging area.

The last facility we will discuss is one that you may or may not ever have to use; you use it only if you need it. This is the **student reunification and release site**. You may not need to release students but if you do, you need to create a physical location where people can come and request their children, present their identification, and allow you to safely transfer custody. This space should be somewhere where the staff has access to the student records, such as their emergency contact forms or their electronic student records and where parents can sign out their kids. It should also be a place where the students and parents cannot have direct contact. This keeps parents who see their children from just walking up and removing the children without anyone on the staff knowing that they are gone!

You will want extra security and helpers at this location to be able to call and have students come from wherever they are waiting for release. It may be an emotional scene depending on the nature of the emergency, but you still have to remember your ultimate responsibility is the safety of the students. Unfortunately, history shows us that sometimes some people attempt to take advantage of the confusion of an evacuation to get away with removing a child that they have no real legal right to remove, such as a parent who no longer has custody. We are still responsible for that student, even more so during an emergency, so we must make sure that we still follow our procedures and you check identification and ensure that the person actually legally can remove the child.

If a police agency is involved in the incident, ask them to supply an extra officer to help with security at the release center. Their presence alone can sometimes keep the group of not-so-patient parents in order while waiting for their kids. Also these officers are usually experienced at looking at legal

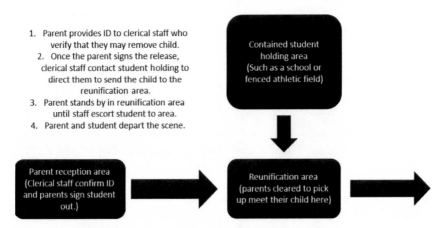

1. Parent provides ID to clerical staff who verify that they may remove child.
2. Once the parent signs the release, clerical staff contact student holding to direct them to send the child to the reunification area.
3. Parent stands by in reunification area until staff escort student to area.
4. Parent and student depart the scene.

Contained student holding area (Such as a school or fenced athletic field)

Parent reception area (Clerical staff confirm ID and parents sign student out.)

Reunification area (parents cleared to pick up meet their child here)

Figure 5.5. Diagram of Student Release and Reunification Site

paperwork and helping determine if someone has a right to take a student or not.

A note here about dealing with anxious parents: remember to have your staff be courteous and try to be understanding. Parents who are coming to a school and finding flashing lights and firefighters or police officers are going to be afraid and nervous because they haven't experienced this before. Try to understand their priority is the same as yours, to ensure that their kids are safe. An old adage that some parents still use is that their kids "aren't safe unless they are in my arms and safe." In the communications chapter we reviewed some of the things that you can do to use communication to avoid some of the issues surrounding this difficult stage of the operation.

There is nothing wrong with that mentality; in fact, it would be great if more parents would feel that way! Sometimes just a gentle reminder that you are being careful so that you can ensure that their kids are safe is the best way to go.

ICS IS ONE SIZE FITS ALL

What do we mean when we say "expandable to meet the needs of any incident"? The system can be used by as few as one person who is performing all of the functions of ICS without even thinking about it. For instance, let's look at a simple classroom fight between two middle school students. The teacher is in the middle of class when two students begin to argue with each other. Soon one is standing up, and the teacher believes they are going to fight. The teacher is the only adult in the room so she is automatically the incident commander. She assesses the situation and walks calmly over to her intercom to press the button. When the office answers, she asks for an administrator to help stopping the fight. This is the communications activity under operations when asking for the additional resources that may be needed.

We can see that she is a one-person ICS. She may be performing different tasks that are broken down by the system. Remember in this way the ICS is an organizational tool. Some people just know what to do; others may have to think. Even one person can think about what needs to be done using the ICS framework in his or her head, operation, planning, and logistics: what has to be done to address the fight, what planning has to be done to get back on track, and what logistical pieces are necessary to do both.

Next she asks the other students to step away but she also looks to make sure that none are out the door. She is taking accountability and assuming the operational responsibility for keeping the other students safe. She may begin

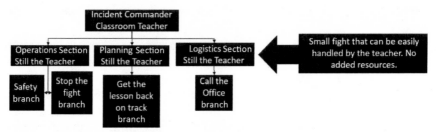

Figure 5.6.   Single Person Organization Chart for Small Fight

to talk to the students and try to separate them before they begin to fight. This is still operations because she is physically trying to do something. If one student strikes another, she may look to see if the student is hurt or call for the nurse, which is the medical part of the operations branch.

Once the students involved have left, she is in the recovery phase and will again use her operational knowledge to return the students to their seats and use her planning hat to get the lesson plan back on track. (Remember that the recovery phase is part of the emergency management cycle, not ICS. We are always in some part of the emergency management cycle, and we are just using incident command when in the response phase and are actually responding to an incident or an emergency.) The terminology may be confusing at first, but the more you practice and work with your emergency plan, the more it will become second nature.

WHAT ABOUT A MORE COMPLICATED
INCIDENT? JUST EXPAND YOUR ICS

You can see how one person can use the ICS as an organizing or "thinking" tool to determine what he or she has to do to ensure that students are safe and an incident is managed effectively. What if the incident requires some help? What if when the teacher looks at certain parts of the ICS, she determines that it would be too much effort for her and she needs to get some help?

The teacher is making the decision based on how many resources would be needed in order to make sure that all the students are safe and the incident is de-escalated. When we add resources, we use a term called "standing up" as in she may need to "stand up" the law enforcement branch because it would only be safe for the school resource officer to manage the fighting students if she could not stop while still ensuring that the other students are safe.

So now her ICS expands to include a person in the operation section for law enforcement. That just takes that aspect of the incident off her plate and gets another resource to manage it. A student got injured? Calling the nurse would "stand up" the medical branch of her ICS, again adding to the resources and reducing the list of things for the teacher, who is still in charge of the classroom, so still the incident commander, and needs to keep in mind. She is still in charge until someone who is higher up in authority arrives and "takes command."

So now an assistant principal shows up, and we change who is in charge. In ICS we call that "passing command." The teacher knows that the incident has grown past where she has enough resources to handle it so she passes control on to the next higher person in experience and authority. Now the teacher will likely become the operations section chief and handle accountability for the safety of the other students.

The AP may ask her to evacuate the classroom by taking the other students into the hall. When the school resource officers (SROs) arrive, they stand up the law enforcement branch of the operations section and assume their role in the ICS. They will be responsible for any physical restraint or arrest that has to be made. Once the nurse gets there, she now becomes the medical branch of the operations section. Now the ICS has expanded from one person to four, but those responsibilities in the ICS have not changed; just now other people are performing them because it is too large an incident to be managed by the single person. It also means that the teacher can change her focus to a more limited role as others start to do their part!

Once the fight is over and the students have been removed, now command passes back and the ICS returns to its normal state with the teacher being the sole ICS in the room because the other resources are no longer needed. As you become more familiar with the system, you will become a real expert at growing it and shrinking the system to meet the needs of the different roles. Each incident requires a different set of responsibilities so you adapt the ICS for the event to include whatever is needed. You may not need a reunification and release branch if you are not dismissing students so there is no need to post someone in operations to that job unless it is needed. The only job that is *always* posted is the incident commander because someone is always in charge during an incident.

Again, it may look complicated in the beginning but remember that with each use you will get more comfortable with the terminology and the use of the ICS organization system and way of thinking. This is just an early example of what it may look like and an easy way to visualize the system. For practice, print several copies of the organization chart from Figure 5.8c and fill them out using different scenarios you may encounter in your school and using your staff to fill in the key roles.

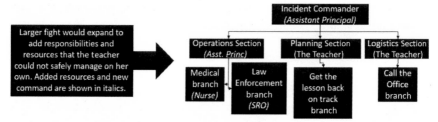

Figure 5.7.   Expanded Organization Chart for Larger Fight

USE THE INCIDENT ACTION PLAN

The incident action plan (IAP) or incident summary is a simple form developed by FEMA for the ICS that is a sort of a one-stop shop for keeping critical information early in an incident. Figure 5.8 is a copy, and after you look at it, we will look at each section.

The first section of the form is a blank open space for you to quickly sketch the area impacted by the incident. If this is a small and relatively straightforward event, you may want to skip this section. However, if you are not positive about the exact location of the issue, have the person who is familiar with the problem draw a diagram so that you can see where it is. It is also handy for people who respond to the command post as a way to direct them to the problem.

The next section asks for a brief note about the situation summary and any health and safety information. This is the area where you quickly jot down what the problem is and what the possible impacts to the student's health and safety. It is a good reminder area to think through not only the situation, but to think about safety.

Next are the few sections that cover the "action" parts of an action plan. This is where you note what the objectives need to be for your incident. Think this through and determine ways with your team to evacuate school, especially your planning section chief. If you are going to evacuate the school, you would make that an objective then break down what tasks you have to do to accomplish them. There is also a section where you can create a timeline for those critical tasks.

The next page shows the all-important organization chart. This all-important chart is not only a great tool for putting names with assignments but thinking through the "who does what." Filling in the blanks based on your incident objectives and the tasks noted in the earlier sections of the form will help you guarantee that you are able to meet all of the perceived demands of the incident. The major parts of the chart are already filled in with your ICS team members.

INCIDENT BRIEFING (ICS 201)

1. Incident Name:	2. Incident Number:	3. Date/Time Initiated: Date: Time:

4. Map/Sketch (include sketch, showing the total area of operations, the incident site/area, impacted and threatened areas, overflight results, trajectories, impacted shorelines, or other graphics depicting situational status and resource assignment):

5. Situation Summary and Health and Safety Briefing (for briefings or transfer of command): Recognize potential incident Health and Safety Hazards and develop necessary measures (remove hazard, provide personal protective equipment, warn people of the hazard) to protect responders from those hazards.

6. Prepared by: Name: _____ Position/Title: _____ Signature: _____
ICS 201, Page 1   Date/Time: _____

Figure 5.8a.   ICS Form 201 Page 1 *Source*: **FEMA.GOV**

The last section is another key tickler for thinking through your plan. This is the list of resources that you need to meet the objectives of the incident. This list is a key for your logistics section chief to try to find those needr resources. It may include things such as school buses or porta potties. T'

INCIDENT BRIEFING (ICS 201)

1. Incident Name:	2. Incident Number:	3. Date/Time Initiated: Date: Time:
7. Current and Planned Objectives:		

8. Current and Planned Actions, Strategies, and Tactics:

Time:	Actions:

6. Prepared by: Name: _____	Position/Title: _____ Signature: _____
ICS 201, Page 2	Date/Time: _____

Figure 5.8b.   ICS Form 201 Page 2 *Source:* **FEMA.GOV**

through the process and try to find resources that align with your complete action plan. Make sure that the resources that you request can be utilized in the organization structure that you have created. This way you will have addressed the people, resources, and tasks that are necessary to get the job done for your school and students!

INCIDENT BRIEFING (ICS 201)

1. Incident Name:	2. Incident Number:	3. Date/Time Initiated: Date: Time:

9. Current Organization (fill in additional organization as appropriate):

```
                              ┌──────────────────────┐
                              │   Liaison Officer     │
        ┌──────────────────┐  ├──────────────────────┤
        │ Incident         │  │   Safety Officer      │
        │ Commander(s)     │  ├──────────────────────┤
        │                  │  │ Public Information    │
        └──────────────────┘  │ Officer               │
                              └──────────────────────┘

┌──────────────┐ ┌──────────────┐ ┌──────────────┐ ┌──────────────┐
│ Planning     │ │ Operations   │ │ Finance/     │ │ Logistics    │
│ Section Chief│ │ Section Chief│ │ Administration│ │ Section Chief│
│              │ │              │ │ Section Chief │ │              │
└──────────────┘ └──────────────┘ └──────────────┘ └──────────────┘
```

6. Prepared by: Name: _____ Position/Title: _____ Signature: _____
ICS 201, Page 3   Date/Time: _____

Figure 5.8c.   ICS Form 201 Page 3 *Source*: **FEMA.GOV**

Now if at all possible make copies of your IAP and distribute it to the other members of the ICS team and staff members that are assigned to roles in the designated organization structure. This way they all will be aware of all of the background issues as well as the resource plan and be aware of what each section and branch is doing. More information is

INCIDENT BRIEFING (ICS 201)

1. Incident Name:		2. Incident Number:			3. Date/Time Initiated: Date: Time:	

10. Resource Summary:

Resource	Resource Identifier	Date/Time Ordered	ETA	Arrived	Notes (location/assignment/status)
				☐	
				☐	
				☐	
				☐	
				☐	
				☐	
				☐	
				☐	
				☐	
				☐	
				☐	
				☐	
				☐	
				☐	
				☐	
				☐	
				☐	

6. Prepared by: Name: _____ Position/Title: _____ Signature: _____	
ICS 201, Page 4	Date/Time: _____

Figure 5.8d.   ICS Form 201 Page 4 *Source*: **FEMA.GOV**

always better than less. It may also assist if someone sees another group doing something dangerous to know what they were supposed to be doing in the first place. Knowing where people are supposed to be and what they are supposed to be doing is yet another form of accountability and it will make for a safer operation and protect the lives and safety of your team and students.

PUTTING IT ALL TOGETHER

How do you make sure that the team is ready? Do they wait until the bell rings to assume their roles? Do you decide as the alarm sounds who does what? Do they change roles depending on the nature of the incidents? All are very good questions, and only you can really answer them because each school is different. Best practices would have you ensure that they are all trained in ICS using the Federal Emergency Management Agency training modules for ICS in schools. As far as when they assume their roles, it is best if they are in the same role in the team at all times so that they get a sense of ownership in their role and will become adept at applying their specific skills in each event. A quick search of the web for "ICS job task sheets" can get you some good customizable forms for your ICS team to use. Remember our play example? You do not decide who is going to play Romeo five minutes before the curtain goes up!

When is the best time to use the team? The answer here is anytime! As described in chapter 1, there are different types of issues that ICS can help you manage from life-threatening emergencies to incidents which impact your learning environment. All could use the system to best meet the needs of the students in your care. This is one reason that it is best to choose team members that do not have direct responsibility for students, so that they are available at a moment's notice to actively participate in your incident. If you have to wait for some other staff member to relieve them in their classroom, precious time can be lost in getting the entire team focused on the mission at hand.

There will also be a need to train backup personnel in the event that the primary person is not at work or is off property for training and so on. Each team member should know his or her alternate and should advise the person in advance that he or she is not available, as well as notify the rest of the ICS team. Then when the alarm sounds, alternates already know that they are up to bat and the rest of the team know who will show up and assume those key roles.

LESSONS LEARNED

- Incident command is an organizational system designed to help you manage any incident using the same structure and skills.
- ICS helps you remember what tasks are important and when it is important to assign someone to do them.
- Operations section members physically do things during an incident. They search, they take accountability of students, and they work with the fire

department to address facility issues. They are the part of the ICS which gets things done.
- The planning team is the "what is next" part of the incident. They look at what is going on and begin to come up with a plan.
- The logistics section works on what resources are available and what resources are needed to meet the needs of the incident. They work with the planning section to come up with a resource plan that meets the goals set by the ICS team.
- ICS can be used by one person as an organizational tool for managing a small incident and expanded as new people and resources are needed for more complex incidents.

Chapter 6

Is It an Incident or Emergency?

THE IMPORTANCE OF SIZE-UP

One of the first things that we need to teach a new administrator is to understand the difference between an emergency and an incident. We define an incident as anything that disrupts the normal operation of the school day but does not affect the immediate health and safety of the students. That's it. It really does sound simple, doesn't it? Well good, because it should sound simple.

The more complex we make the decision-making process, the harder it is to apply when we need to. Keep it simple. Are kids safe or not? If they are safe, then what's next? Can they learn or not? Answer those two questions and you are well on your way to being an excellent incident commander.

Here's a quick example. Imagine an issue that involved water becoming trapped in a Dumpster along with some waste from the cafeteria during an extremely hot spring. When you arrive at the school in question, the odor is clearly causing a significant problem. Even the birds that usually hang around the Dumpster have taken off for better smelling trash!

Clearly, students are not going to be able to learn in this environment. You know that you either have to move the students to another school or cancel the school day because it is impossible for them to learn.

This is considered an incident since the students' lives are not in danger nor are there any risks to the students' safety and health. The students just would have been too bothered by the smell to learn math that day. You still had to act, but not necessarily as quickly or with as many resources as you would have in the case of a true emergency. It meant that our team could take its time and really plan, determining what resources we needed and assembling them rather than jumping right into action. One of the things about size-up is it can open or close the window of time you have to make decisions. The less life-threatening, the more time to make well-planned decisions.

It's important to determine early on whether you're responding to an incident or to an emergency. One reason why this decision is a key factor is the timing and the amount of resources that are necessary.

If we are faced with an emergency, we have to make decisions quickly and efficiently in order to ensure the safety of the students. If we're encountering an incident, we may have a little bit of time to ensure that we're making the most effective decisions to address the issue. In an emergency we want to bring as many resources as necessary to ensure the safety of the students in a very rapid and efficient fashion. There really is no time for mistakes when student safety is involved.

ASSESSING THE LEVEL OF RISK

One of the most important things that you as a new administrator can do is to learn how to look at a situation based on the level of risk involving the students and staff. In the earlier trash odor example, we decided this issue was not a life-threatening emergency. While we could have called the fire department to get help, we did not order an emergency evacuation of the school. In fact, we took time to make decisions as an ICS team since no one's life was in danger.

After you have established whether the incident is an emergency, you should begin to look at the nature of the impact:

- Are all of the students and school impacted by the incident?
- Does it only impact small number of students? Is the incident limited to a certain geographic area of the school?
- How severe is the impact?

Let's look at another example, such as having water issues in your school. Say you have to shut the water off to the second floor of a three-story school. This is not an emergency; you can redirect students and staff to utilize facilities and other parts of the school. It is an incident that will require you to plan in order to ensure that students are safely and efficiently monitored and moved to utilize facilities and other locations.

It is also important for the school administrator to realize that his or her definition of an incident versus an emergency may be different from that of some of the other members of the staff. It is not unusual for some staff members to decide that something is absolutely a life-threatening emergency and possess "Sky is Falling Syndrome." Part of our role as the school leader and the incident commander is to help communicate our confidence in our ability to manage the incident.

We will discuss the communications aspect more in a later chapter, but it is an important focus of the first few minutes of an incident. Having a single staff member who is contributing to panic and not helping the students to remain calm is detrimental to the overall effectiveness of any incident operation. It is imperative that staff members are reminded that their role is always to be calm and to follow the instructions of the ICS team.

It is very important for the incident commander to always maintain a calm and in-control attitude. Even while evaluating whether an incident is turning into an emergency, the administrator needs to remain calm and be comforting to those that they encounter. This can be particularly important if it really turns out to be an emergency. If a student has been injured and the principal, administrator, or teacher appears to lose control and become visibly upset, the student who is experiencing the medical emergency may also become upset, which can worsen his or her medical condition. In these situations, school leaders must appear cool, calm, and collected.

For example, an emergency medical technician on an ambulance always uses a calm voice when talking to patients whether they are conscious or unconscious. It is their way to ensure their patients that the person taking care of them is in control and is going to actually help.

In much the same way a school administrator who is monitoring the medical emergency must act as if he or she is in total control and the student is going to be fine. As you become more experienced in incident command, you will notice that your calm demeanor is contagious and other staff members will attempt to remain calm in order to imitate your appearance.

RESOURCES, PLANS, AND MANAGEMENT STRATEGIES

Once we determine that any issue is a true emergency, we need to begin marshaling resources and creating a plan to quickly and efficiently manage the situation. Note the phrase "manage the situation," not "respond to the situation" or "let the situation decide what we're going to do." There's a mind-set here, the mind-set that *we* are going to manage the situation and not the other way around.

While it's true that we cannot tell the fire to go out, we certainly can take positive steps to ensure an effective evacuation of all of the staff and students. We can manage our end of the operation. We muster our ICS team and get them working on developing our plan. One of the things we focus our efforts on is planning to stay one step ahead of the incident. That is why it is so important to have an organized team and not just one person responding to each individual crisis that comes across the radio.

Throughout this book we will repeatedly return to the principle of knowing where students are and that they are safe. The fire department will put the fire out, the police department will handle any police action, and the maintenance department will take care of any damage to our school. They all have their responsibilities, but none of them have the responsibility for the ultimate safety of the students. That is always our primary mission.

So now that you have established that we are faced with an emergency, you need to very quickly decide what immediate steps are necessary to ensure the safe accountability of all of our students. Many of us will believe that evacuation is always the first step in student safety. But that's not always the case. For instance, if faced with a gas leak outside of the school the safest place may not be outside the school in the area of the leaking gas. That's why understanding the nature of the situation is important.

Let's look at a gas leak from the very beginning as a potential emergency. Let's suppose that a teacher in the rear of your school notifies the office that she believes she smells gas. A custodian and the school administrator respond to the classroom, and indeed they smell what appears to be a natural gas. A quick check of classrooms close to this class reveals that all the classes at the rear of the school appear to have an odor of gas.

As the administrator you decide to send a custodian outside to see if the gas is present outside or inside the school. Once outside your custodian determines that the gas leak is in the rear of the school. At this time what would you do?

You have a couple options, but the first thing would be to notify the fire department. These folks are the people who respond to these types of emergencies and you're going to need their help very quickly. The next decision is whether we evacuate the students or not. If the threat is outside where the leak is located, should we evacuate them to the outside of the school? Suppose we determine that the wind is blowing from the front of the school toward the back?

The gas leak that is outside is blowing away from the school in the rear. Now we can begin discussing removing students to the front of the school and away from a hazard. Notice we didn't just pull the fire alarm and evacuate all the students. If we did that, this would not only lead to evacuation of students to the area where the leak exists, but we have the possibility that some of that movement could lead to triggering an explosion involving that gas. Now, that is the worst-case scenario, but it is still possible to manage if we consider the incident command.

So now we have our resources on the way and we've taken steps to ensure that the students are accounted for and safe away from the hazard. Congratulations you just talked your way through your very first emergency as incident commander. It gets much easier from here!

Once you become familiar with ways to evaluate the nature and severity of an incident or emergency, you will quickly become adept at applying the principles of incident management to each different situation. After you have read this book, you will see that there are plenty of resources and tried and true methods to help you and your staff accomplish your number-one mission of keeping kids safe! This scenario will come back in more detail later in the book as we look at using the incident command tools to really effectively manage this same incident.

MAKE SIZE-UP DECISION MAKING A HABIT

Regardless of the nature of the incident or emergency, you can utilize the very same sort of size-up technique. In the earlier chapter we talked about asking yourself questions such as, is this a life-threatening problem, does it impact the entire school population, or is it limited to one geographic location within our building? Those questions can be answered regardless of the nature of the emergency. So you should get into the habit of asking yourself those questions first anytime you're evaluating whether you're handling an emergency or an incident and you begin thinking about the types of resources you may need to address the issue.

CALL IN THE CAVALRY!

Another topic that we will explore repeatedly as you continue to develop your skills as an incident commander is the ability to determine how much help you need and how quickly you will need it. Resources are often a key to managing any situation, and you should also learn to *always* have more help than you think you need in order to effectively manage an incident. In the fire service, new leaders are taught to always call for the cavalry; you can always send them home if you don't need them, but you are out of luck if you need help quickly and you didn't call to get it!

Sometimes we have heard discussions about principals who call 9-1-1 and get the fire department to the school too often. In this expert's opinion, that is ridiculous! They are there to help, so use them—if for no other reason than it gets them familiar with your school and your incident command team. In my own experience with the fire service, they were never upset or even bothered by having to go to a school for a "false alarm." It usually turned into a fun chance for the students to check out a fire engine, so we made the visit into a fire prevention activity.

LESSONS LEARNED

- One of the first pieces of information you need to do as a school administrator/incident commander is to size up an issue.
- An emergency is anything that threatens the lives and safety of our students.
- An incident is any event that impacts the student's ability to learn or disrupts the normal operation of a school.
- Another important aspect of a size-up is determining how many students or what parts of the school are directly impacted by the incident or emergency.
- Once you decide that there is an emergency, you should quickly request resources to help you manage the emergency.
- As the school and ICS team leader you should always maintain a calm and reassuring appearance. It is important that everyone knows that the person in charge is in control.
- Do not make rash decisions or rush decisions. Before you take an action, consider the possible impacts. What you have always done in an emergency may not be the best, or safest, thing to do.

Chapter 7

Putting All the Pieces Together in an Incident Action Plan

WHAT? *ANOTHER* GAS LEAK?

Well, no, we never really *stopped* the one discussed earlier—we just talked about it. This time, now that you are familiar with ICS and what each aspect of it addresses, we will go through the same scenario, but apply the tools and resources from ICS. Begin the scenario with the discovery of the gas smell by your staff. You would quickly muster your trained and ready ICS team.

Now you would begin looking at the situation in terms of the breakdown of your ICS components: operations, planning, and logistics. Your operations folks in this case would be those custodians that you sent out earlier to check for the location of the smell. While this is occurring, your planning and logistics chiefs will begin with the basics: how many students and staff are here and if they have to evacuate, where would they all fit? While the three ICS team members are doing their jobs, the fire department is also on the way.

The operations team reports that the gas smell is strong outside and the fire department has arrived. A fire chief makes his way to your conference room command post and lets you know that there is a major gas line rupture in the area and you are going to have to evacuate the school for the safety of all of the students.

SIZE-UP AND INCIDENT ACTION PLAN DEVELOPMENT

In this case, your size-up is pretty well complete. You know that the gas leak is far beyond your scope of control and that you will have to evacuate the school. The fire chief is an impromptu part of your ICS team. This would be a good time to ask his advice on where around the school would be safe to stage buses to get the students out to a safe location. He can quickly work with your operations chief to find that location while your logistics chief begins to work with your transportation shop to get buses rolling to your location. Your planning chief can begin calling the location designated in your evacuation plan as your off-site evacuation location to make sure that they are aware that you are coming. Your district office may also be involved in helping with this aspect of the operation.

So without even really thinking about it, you have already created the outline of an incident action plan (IAP)! Your overall objective will be to safely and quickly evacuate all students to your off-site location without exposing them to the outside conditions around the gas leak. The tasks required to achieve this objective include staging buses for an orderly and controlled evacuation, ensuring that students with health risks are evaluated and evacuated first then all others in order of risk, ensuring that the off-site location is prepared to receive your students, and taking the steps necessary to maintain accountability at departure and arrival at the other site.

Now would be a great time to use the organization chart in the IAP to find staff members to assume key responsibilities that you have determined are needed. We know based on our objectives that we need to accomplish certain things. Always first is to maintain accountability so we will need people to load the buses and verify who is on them when they leave and someone else at the evacuation site must be there to receive them and verify that they arrived. We need people to help efficiently load the students, and we will need people to help manage the flow of those buses as they arrive so we avoid chaos. The chart may look like the one shown in figure 7.1.

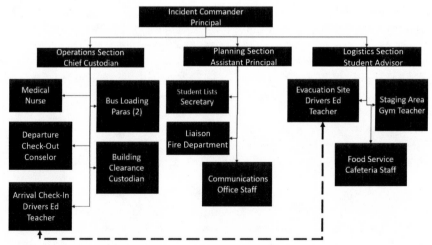

Figure 7.1. Possible Organization Chart for Gas Leak Evacuation

Let's break down each section and what their folks will be doing during this emergency if we are using the IAP and the organization chart.

- *Operations Section:* The chief custodian is trained to oversee this section. He will make sure that two paraprofessionals are standing by at the designated student exit to help load students onto the buses as they arrive from the staging area. The school's guidance counselor is responsible for taking the names of each teacher that gets their class on the bus and for verifying how many students from each class are on each bus before they depart for the off-site location. The school nurse must be available to responds if there is a medical issue during the process.

At the off-site location, the drivers ed teacher that headed over earlier from the logistics section in order to make sure they know where the students are headed will now join the operations section as the person who meets each bus as they arrive and does the exact same check in as the bus did when they left your school, list each teacher's class that is on the bus and how many students from each class arrive. They will then work with the off-site location to ensure that they know where each bus's load is being located inside the location.

Lastly the other custodians may help with getting the students out to the buses and then will use their knowledge of the school to inspect it to make sure the students and staff are all safely away before securing the school and departing themselves.

- *Planning Section:* The assistant principal is in charge of this section. He or she will work with the office staff to accomplish most of the accountability planning for this evacuation. Your school secretary will make sure that she grabs their main school lists and attendance roster if it is available. They may need to bring a laptop to the off-site location to help make sure that they have the records necessary to dismiss students to their parents if they are dismissed from the other site.

The office staff will also be responsible for gathering portable radios to bring to the off-site location. Communications is always a key, and it is far better to bring your own radios that your staff is familiar with than to try to piece together free radios at another school or worse an outside agency.

- *Logistics Section:* In this case a student advisor has been trained to assume this key role in the ICS staff. One of the most important aspects of this section during this emergency will be operating the staging area; the gym teacher has been given a radio and sent to the street where the fire department recommends, and the buses wait to come into the area to load students. As the bus loading branch tells him that a bus has departed, he will send the next ready bus out of the staging area to the school to begin loading. A drivers ed teacher early on will head over to the off-site evacuation site to make sure that he knows where the buses will arrive and release students and into which area of the location will the students be sent.

After they have established that information and sent it back to the incident commander who can share it with the operations section so that they can let the buses departing know, the drivers ed teacher will take a note of the arriving buses and verify their information as they arrive. The cafeteria staff is also a part of the logistics section. If possible, they can be sent to the off-site location to help prepare a meal or snack for the displaced students as they await the decision to dismiss or whatever occurs next in their hectic day.

MONITOR THE PLAN IMPLEMENTATION AND CHANGE AS NEEDED

Now that you have developed the plan and put it into action, you need to monitor it and make sure that it is occurring safely and efficiently. Remember the reason that we use such a system as ICS to make sure that we are using resources efficiently. Keep checking to make sure that the buses are moving from staging area to the school and departing to the off-site location quickly. If there is a delay, see where additional resources may be needed to help smooth the flow. It may be possible to load two buses at a time which would effectively reduce the amount of time of the evacuation in half.

As all of the buses arrive at the site, a simple text message or cell phone call from the off-site team to the IC will help keep the command post aware of how much progress they made and how much work is left. While it may have only taken a few minutes to develop the plan, it may take a half an hour to an hour to accomplish the goals in the plan. You really are dependent on the number of buses available and other outside issues such as traffic in the area and the impact of the gas leak which is forcing you to evacuate in the first place.

FOLLOW THROUGH UNTIL ALL OF THE PLAN'S OBJECTIVES ARE MET OR THE EMERGENCY IS UNDER CONTROL

So once you have successfully moved all of the students to the off-site location and they are all accounted for, you have met all of the goals set up in your IAP. Now you can begin the next steps in the planning process. Obviously it's still not over. Now you will have to figure out the next steps in a new IAP! Either students will have to be dismissed from this new location, or you will be returning to your school; either way you will need to go through the exact same process to develop new goals and objectives for that next phase of your incident! There is always a "what's next!"

LESSONS LEARNED

- Once you have a good working knowledge of using ICS, you will naturally and automatically start moving through the process as a team when incidents occur.
- Start by using size-up to determine the severity and impact of the emergency.
- Once you know what the problem is, use the IAP to determine what your priorities are and what tasks need to be accomplished to meet those goals.
- After you have implemented the plan, you must keep monitoring it.
- If the plan is working slowly or not effectively, use the planning process to find resources or different methods to increase your efficiency.

Chapter 8

Decision-Making Tools

THINKING IS THE MOST IMPORTANT
PART OF COMMAND

Let's look at decision making as a separate entity in the realm of emergency management. It is a skill set that will help you in all of the different aspects of your personal and professional life, but you really have to hone those skills if you are going to be an effective incident commander and leader. Your goal is to make quick, effective, *and* defendable decisions. When your decisions apply all three concepts, then you are generally on very solid ground for being an effective decision maker. If you are lacking in any one of them, then like a three-legged stool, your decision making process may fall down.

Look at the first aspect of the three, the *quick* part. Everyone has a different definition of quick, but you can generally see for yourself how long it is taking you if everyone is standing there and staring at you for a decision before they do anything, then it is taking too long. Remember there are *always* things that we can have our team doing to manage an incident so having them sit there while you consider your options may not be the best use of resources.

That doesn't mean you have to rush critical decisions. If there is not a clear choice that stands out as the right thing to do, ask questions and make sure you have all the information that you need. Just remember that time is not a luxury when an incident is occurring so try to turn around your answers as quickly as you can.

Next we come to *effective*. This is another subjective one, but you can use some of your training as an educator to help. Remember when they taught you to use the "SMART" goal system for determining what your students can learn in a given period? The "A" stood for achievable. If we decide to do something that clearly would stretch the limits of your staff's ability or is simply not plausible with the resources that you have, you are making an ineffective decision.

They need to be achievable, and staff members need to know what you expect to be the result of their effort specifically. Giving an ambiguous command such as "clear the school" could have different meanings to different people and does not set a definite objective. Does it mean clear everyone from inside or just check for students? Does it include people who are in the area of the school but not inside? If I finish checking one part, I have to assume that someone may have come in the part that I already checked so then I have to go back. All those thoughts would bounce around.

So how do we capture that same task in an effective way? "Operations from Command: clear the lower level first and take some caution tape. When you enter the floor put the tape across the door so that people know they should not enter and check it to the other end and do the same thing with the tape." Then come back and we can assign you another floor to check. That is effective and it gives them specific direction and leaves little room for ambiguity.

Finally, you must look at defendable decisions. This can be the toughest one of all. In our society every time we make a decision we will be second guessed by our bosses, by parents, by teachers, and by the media. All of these folks, after the incident is over, will come back to you and say, "Why did you decide that?" And you have to have an answer. You may end up in a court of law and have a jury of your peers (who are not really your peers because none of them have ever been a school leader or been in command at an incident in a school) and have to explain them why you decided what you decided.

So what makes a decision defendable? Well I am glad you asked that question! The answer really is quite simple: make decisions that you believe will make the kids safer than they are right now. If you are looking at a decision and saying "if I do that, it puts the kids in harm's way," then you really will not be able to defend it.

Let's use an example of a light ballast that smells really bad when it burns out. Many of you have experienced this in your older schools, and it is just another issue that happens. So your chief custodian comes to you and says that the lights flickered in the cafeteria and you smell the smoke, and he thinks it was just a ballast and will call your maintenance folks. You go to check it out and you too can smell the smell of an electrical component that seems to have burned up. You cannot see the ballast because it is above the ceiling but you sure smell it.

Now let's think from a defendable stand point. So you are left to decide what to do. Your chief thinks nothing of it, it has happened before. But your chief is not responsible for the lives of the students. Ask yourself "am I an electrician and do I really know for sure what that smell is?" The answer is more likely "no." Can I be sure that there is no fire up there and no risk to the students? Again, really no. Heaven forbid it is more than a ballast and you decided to sit around and wait for maintenance.

So, you decide to air on the safe side. "Chief we haven't had our fire drill this month, let's go ahead and get the kids out and have the fire department come clear it just to be on the safe side," you say in the form of your effective, timely, and defendable decision. The fire department *can* determine if it was just a ballast and when they say it is safe to go back inside it is not the opinion of a principal but the opinion of a fire expert that you are good to go. If anyone asks, you decided to be 100 percent sure the kids were safe rather than risk it.

APPLYING THE OODA LOOP

The OODA loop is another tool to add to your decision-making toolbox. The OODA was created by a fighter pilot, Air Force Colonel John Lloyd, who tried to find a quick tool to use while engaged in air combat. After all, at several hundred miles an hour decisions have to be made quickly because everything happens quickly! The letters stand for Observe, Orient, Decide, and Act.

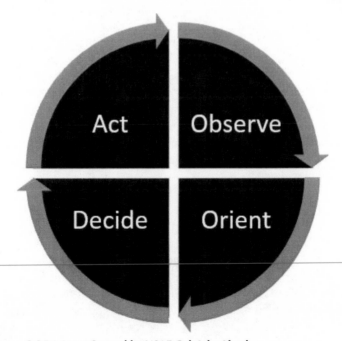

Figure 8.1. OODA Loop Created by USAF Col. John Lloyd

Start with the *observe*. It means looking at all of the information that presents itself to you. Try to avoid seeking more information than what you see. You do not need to know everything that would take time, which would make it harder to make a quick decision right? Glad you agree!

Next comes *orient*. This means to add context. That could be pretty difficult in an emergency because we are not looking at normal information. In the most extreme circumstances we may be talking about acts of violence. Our normal mind may have difficulty processing that type of information so we must prepare ourselves in advance for it. We must remember that we may be orienting ourselves to the worst possible information. So we are taking what we see and orienting it based on our knowledge. If we are looking at our school from a physical standpoint, we may be orienting ourselves in a direction and applying our knowledge. If we hear the sound of gunfire from a certain direction, we may orient ourselves based on what we know is down in that direction.

Next comes the "D" for *decide*. You now make a decision based on your observations and orientation. Deciding is where the priorities we looked at before come into play. So if you hear gunshots from an area you believe is the gym and you have some students with you, you may decide to make sure the students get away from the danger area. So your decision may be direct them to run and call 9-1-1 from outside of the school (if they are high school students, you wouldn't do that if they were in first grade!)

Finally, we arrive at the "A" for *act*. That is where you put your decision into action. You ask if one of the students has a cell phone and you send them on their way. So you used the "OODA" loop to make a quick decision. Now you can just sit back and congratulate yourself on a job well done, right? That would be a great big no! There is still an emergency and still more decisions to be made so you go right back to the first "O" and do it all over again. You will keep the incident command decision-making toolbox open for the remainder of the incident, dipping in and using the different tools we reviewed until the incident comes to an end and you get to go home and get ready for the next incident!

REMEMBER YOUR PRIORITIES

Remember that at every stage of the decision-making process we also must focus on our priorities. Our two goals are to know where all of the students are and that they are safe. So what if one of the students has been injured? Then our goal is that no others get injured and that we prevent further injury to the one who gets hurt. The goals do not really change; we just focus our decisions on the two priorities.

We have all taken hours and hours of leadership classes and professional development focused on ethical decision making. These classes generally taught us to use our value systems to make critical decisions and that would assist you in also making ethical decisions (assuming that your values were also ethical!). So now you are applying the same concept to your decision making during an incident. You are using your primary objectives in place of your value system, so you are thinking about accountability and keeping kids safe.

So how will that work if someone is injured? Well the same applies; try to keep them from becoming *more* injured or to keep others from getting injured. It may help to think like a parent. After all, you are filling in for them. What would they think about? They would consider minimizing how hurt their child is and getting them medical attention! Sounds like a pretty solid and defendable decision-making plan doesn't it? Can you think of any reason why it wouldn't be a great basis for a decision? Good, because neither could any other reasonable person!

Next we need to remember the order of priority of the people involved. Who is the most important person to focus on when we are making these decisions? Almost every one of you probably just said out loud, "the kids of course!" And, of course, you are right. Let's look at another part of the tool-box, another military tool called the "Three Ms of the Mission." That stands for "Mission, the Men and Me." That means when you are applying your priorities you are also applying them in order of importance, focusing on the mission, then the men, and finally yourself.

The mission is simple; it is our job to protect the lives of the children who are entrusted to our care. Next comes the "men" part. Now before readers jump through the book asking about the gender specificity, it came from the men as in the people of the military, in old combat units they were men. (Besides if it were broken down into the three M, FM, Ms then it would be confusing and harder to remember!) This means our second priority is focusing on the safety and protection of our staff.

Why does the last M stand for "me?" Simply put, you should never place your own concerns above those of the other two groups. The reason is simple; it becomes a concern about placing your own best interest above the interest of others. You could be tired; you could be afraid of what may happen to you after the incident is over. Just remember that most parents would never worry about themselves when the safety of their children is at stake. As school leaders, you assume the same responsibility. Forget the politics or the possible repercussions—always focus on the kids and your staff. (Want to read more about the concept? Check out leadership expert Simon Sinek's book, *Why Leaders Eat Last*.)

We look at decisions in life based on positives and negatives, right? Have you ever taken a sheet of paper and written down a list of good things that could come from a decision and compared them to the list of bad things? In business they call this a "cost-benefit analysis." You are essentially doing the same thing. What does it cost for the fire department to come? Nothing, they are free. We lose a little class time, but we also have to do one fire drill per month. Oh and by the way, the last thing on our benefit list is that all the kids are safe. There can be no cost ever that is greater than the safety of a student.

In the communications chapter we will discuss some more about how important it is to share your reasoning behind making decisions that impact the safety of students based on ensuring the safety of students. Remember our mantra: parents worry far less about their child's education than they do about their child's safety.

So now let's touch on another sometimes difficult topic: when someone from the district office disagrees with you. This can be a touchy subject, especially when you are a relatively new administrator. Just remember that these folks usually spend most of their time doing the same thing you are trying to do, make defendable decisions. Make sure that when they show up at your incident, take a minute to brief them, and do not just share what you are doing, but the "why" behind your defendable decisions. No one has ever met a district administrator who can argue with the words, "I felt it was the safest thing to do for the students."

While we discussed writing down lists of positives and negatives, remember we are talking about timely decisions, so we usually do not have time to write them down during an incident. However, when the incident is over, document what you did and why you did it. What information were you given, and how did that impact your decision-making process? Be aware that we may end up in court a few months or years after an incident and our memory will not remember everything that everyone said or that we saw that day. Better to write it down and keep it fresh in your mind. Then when the time comes that you need to answer questions, you can refresh your memory by looking at your notes. Also use the forms in the ICS to help.

LESSONS LEARNED

- Decisions should be timely, effective, and defendable.
- Make sure your decisions and directions are specific and achievable. They must have an end and everyone knows when the task is finished.
- Defendable decisions always take the view that student safety is the biggest factor, so if the decision may not make the kids any safer than they are right now, it is *not* a defendable decision.
- Use the OODA loop as you look at a situation and need to make a decision. Observe, Orient, Decide, and Act.

- The three "Ms" is a good tool for setting priorities: *Mission, the men, then me*. The "mission" is keeping students safe, the "men" is keeping your staff safe, and lastly you can worry about yourself.
- Always remember that your decisions must be defendable in the eyes of the parents, the press, and possibly in court. View things through their lens: would they think that a decision makes sense?
- You may not have time to write down your thinking during the incident, but you have time after the incident and you should document why you set the course of action that you did. You never know when you may need the information!

Chapter 9

Staging Area Management

STAGING AREA: KEY TO RESOURCE MANAGEMENT

One of the best ways to successfully manage your incident scene is by effectively using the staging area. Remember the staging area is like the backstage of your play. It is a place where you store all the props and actors that are not being used on stage. For us, the staging area is where you send resources and personnel that you are not using to manage the incident. Let's check out an example.

Imagine that a school located in a small city had to be evacuated to another location. The school requires many more buses than it normally requires because the walkers and car riders as well as the students who normally ride the bus need to be moved! The buses will clearly not fit in front of the school. What will we do? We need to find a place nearby to have the buses wait and be able to use each one when we need them.

So once we find a place, how do we get the buses to our location? We have to assign a person using our ICS. That becomes the role of the staging area manager. Make sure the manager has a radio and is communicating with the operations chief back at the school. When each bus is filled and departs, the operations chief will call the staging area manager on the radio and ask for the next ready bus to head to the school. It is that simple.

This type of location saves confusion in the school area. If you have too many people and too many vehicles in front of your school or hanging around your command post, this is a large problem, especially if there are resources that you did not ask for but showed up to help. You may need some help, but they might be getting in the way at the scene. The staging area is a great place to have them sent so that the staging area manager knows where they are in case the command post asks for them.

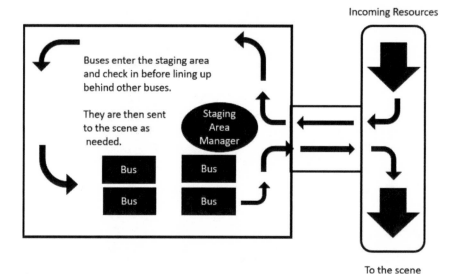

Incoming Resources

To the scene

Figure 9.1. A Staging Area for Staging Buses during a Student Evacuation

LOCATION, LOCATION, LOCATION

We need to pick a location that should be easily accessed by different vehicles heading our way. How will we know what kind of vehicles and how many? You can look at the nature of the incident. For example, in the school evacuation case, we know we need a large enough parking area that can support large school buses. What about a large-scale medical emergency? Then you may need a closer location that can accommodate smaller vehicles such as ambulances. You would need a much smaller parking area.

In addition to having enough room to accommodate vehicles at the staging area, you need to consider how easily and quickly they can respond from the staging area to the school. This may be a great task to request assistance from the police. If possible, they should shut down the roadway between your staging area and the school so that vehicles can quickly move from staging area to the scene without delay.

Your staging area should be designed so that your staging area manager is near the exit of the area, and all of the drivers and personnel waiting there are in communication with the staging manager. They should *not* be able to call the command post directly. Why, you may wonder? Remember that we always focus on accountability, knowing where everyone is at all times. Also recall that one of the important aspects of the ICS is the focus on limiting the span of control. If there are thirteen buses in the staging area and another seven at the school, it would exceed the span of control for the operations chief at the scene. There would be confusion over which buses were located where and how they were being used.

It is very important for the staging area manager to be aware of the location for all of the drivers and resources at all times during the operation. When the command post calls for one of the resources to be sent to the scene, it is imperative that resource is being dispatched immediately. Once the resource leaves of the staging area, the staging area manager must notify the command post that the resource is on the way. If the resource is to go to a specific area or report to a specific person, that information should be relayed to the driver before it leaves the staging area to minimize interruption once he or she arrives at the scene.

This is also the transition time. Once the bus leaves the staging area, it becomes a responsibility of the operations chief. The staging manager is only responsible for maintaining control over the resources in the staging area. After the buses completed its run, if it is still available, they can return to the staging area and can be ready for another run if needed. This same thought process goes along with other resources that may be assigned to staging.

For instance, if an ambulance takes a patient to a hospital, after it has completed its hospital run, it would return to staging area to stand by for the next emergency. This aspect of the operation is very important. Resources that bypass staging can create traffic concerns and "clutter" the scene while making accountability of available resources difficult.

CAN "PEOPLE" BE A RESOURCE AT THE STAGING AREA?

The simple answer is yes; people are resources as well and they should be directed to the staging area rather than sent right to the command post unless they were asked specifically to come into the scene. Some examples may be relief equipment operators if there is heavy equipment being operated or relief firefighters. If your school is being used as an evacuation center, there may be relief workers coming in to assist with the victims. Even food service staff who are being sent to supply food or water to the staff and students should go to the staging area so that the command post can decide when and where the food service staff can best be used.

If the people come without a vehicle, you may need a van or bus as a place to keep individuals out of the elements and comfortable until they are needed. This may also be a good place to keep drivers of vehicles in staging in one place so that they can easily be located and given instructions. Usually buses have a radio and give you the chance to use it to communicate with the command post.

CAN YOU "STAGE" RESOURCES WITHOUT A FULL STAGING AREA?

Not only can you stage resources without standing up your full off-site staging area, but you will use this stepped-down model of staging far more frequently. Sometimes you simply do not need a full staging area, but you need to keep people and vehicles from creating a traffic hazard or simply cluttering up your scene.

In cases like this you may contact resources before they arrive or send someone out to the road before your entrance to stop incoming resources before they turn in. Have them turn on their four-way flashers and simply wait. If they aren't needed, you can release them and they can continue right down the road. If you may need a few of them to come into the scene, just request the equipment that you need to come in and the rest stay where they are.

The fire department will often use this method. Fire apparatus can be big and cumbersome, so it is easier to leave the big hook and ladder truck out on the road rather than trying to navigate our parking lots unless we really need them. Sometimes we may even see the engine (the one with the water and hoses on it) stop at the nearest fire hydrant and just wait there. What are they waiting for? They are "staging" at the hydrant in case they need to attach their hoses to it and fight a real fire.

This would include resources such as your maintenance electricians. If the fire department is still on scene, ask the fire chief if they need the electrician or not. If not, ask them to stage away from the school until they are called. This way you will control the flow of vehicles and people on your emergency scene until those resources are needed.

LESSONS LEARNED

- The staging area is a great place to keep resources that are not needed at the scene.
- A staging area manager must be able to communicate with the command post as well as all of the drivers and resources in the staging area.
- The staging area needs to have enough room to allow vehicles to enter and leave in an organized way.
- You can still "stage" resources on the main road by your school's entrance if you do not need them in the scene.

Chapter 10

Getting Help from the Outside World

There are a multitude of other agencies that can become very useful to you during an incident. The time to get to know these resources and how to contact them is not the day of an incident, but during your work in the mitigation phase. As you look at what you need or could use during an incident, look at what others provide that may be useful. Remember it is not a bad idea to have a list of outside agencies and their contact information even if you never use them!

PUBLIC WORKS

Public work agencies handle your power supply, your telephones, and your water and sewer lines. You never know when an incident may involve one of their crews. For instance, your power and gas utility is incredibly important during a fire emergency where shutting off the flow of gas to your school would be essential to protecting the firefighters and the integrity of the school from an explosion. During the same firefighting operation, the water company may be needed to help in the event there is not enough water to support firefighting activities.

What about the sewer company? Why do we need to know its information? Actually there are several reasons. You could have a sewage blockage leading to an interruption in the sewage leaving the property. While this may not be life-threatening, it surely will be impossible to teach if the smell of raw sewage is floating around the school! You may experience some type of chemical leak and need the sewer company to help protect the sewers from any chemical runoff.

These companies also have some heavy equipment such as front end loaders and high-reach trucks. Need to inspect the roof but cannot access it easily? Contact the power utility to see if one of their trucks can help! Again, one of the benefits to planning is that you get to know what resources other agencies have in case you may need to use them. It is OK to think outside of the box; whatever emergency you are managing certainly doesn't have a box to think inside of so why should you?

IS THAT A FOOD TRUCK COMING ONTO THE SCENE?

The country has been going food truck crazy for several years, and these portable professional kitchens are popping up all over the country. While this may provide a fantastic lunch alternative for your busy staff, it also provides us with an option for logistical support during an incident. Need to feed students and the cafeteria is out of service? If you have met with several food truck vendors, you may be able to scramble a few to quickly meet your needs.

What about the other folks at my emergency scene? You may have staff working after an incident such as district maintenance or fire and water damage restoration contractors. Do you really want them to leave the scene anytime lunch rolls around? Why not provide some food services right on the scene for water and refreshments (or coffee and hot chocolate during winter) as well as food when needed? This will limit the need for outside travel away from your site as well as support the effective recuperation and support of the resources that are operating in your school.

Another good resource is good old-fashioned pizza joints! There are always plenty around, and some may even have contracts with your school already for Friday lunches or specials. If you already have an account, ordering pizza is not a huge deal. Almost everyone likes pizza, and it is portable and low mess kind of food for use during an emergency.

SANITARY SERVICES? WHEN YOU GOTTA GO!

One thing that we all know for sure is everyone needs to use the restroom. If your school's restrooms are out of service and you are in a long-term operation, such as the fire and water restoration we discussed in the earlier example, you may need to bring in porta potties. Folks need to use the bathroom, and if you have the water shut down or there was a leak that interrupted water service, you will need to know whom to get these portable wonders from and in a hurry. If your school is operating as a shelter for community members and the area around your school was impacted, again you would need to call for these facilities.

Having an outdoor event such as a football game and you don't want people coming and going inside your school to use the restrooms? Holding an outdoor graduation at your school? Rent a few and have them placed close to the stadium. Just another resource in your bag of tricks in case you ever need one. Far better to have the information and never need it than to not have it when you are desperate for it.

TRANSPORTATION

We all have access to school buses and that is a great resource. What happens if all of those buses are committed to other school districts or other runs and cannot get to you quickly? What if the weather is hot and you don't have air-conditioned buses and just need a place for students to be kept until arrangements for dismissal can be made? This could be a great time to contact your local public transportation agency.

Most urban and suburban public transportation agencies use air-conditioned buses that people with disability can access. In most cases, they also will have buses that are not in service but can be sent to assist you as a temporary holding facility or even to transport students to another location in the event of an evacuation.

What about the private bus contractors that you use for long-distance field trips? Is there one nearby that would be willing to offer some help if you called? Another advantage to these types of buses is that they have onboard entertainment and lavatory facilities to support longer stays if necessary. Hopefully it would not be necessary but when would the best time to find out if they have resources that you can use? You are right if you said, right now, not when the emergency occurs!

BANQUET FACILITIES, HOTELS, AND LOCAL CHURCHES

All of these places have one thing that may be very helpful during an emergency: a large meeting space. If we have to evacuate and another school is not nearby, perhaps the local church or hotel may be another good resource. Even your local fire company may have a hall that can accommodate a large group of people. If you have an emergency, you can send students to these facilities for a short time until parents can be contacted to come get them.

The time to discover what each of these places has in the way of capacity is now. Call them and see if they would be willing to meet with you and discuss using their business for an emergency. You may not need a formal agreement but may just want to touch base. There will be times when the business has events and cannot accommodate your needs. That is OK, options are always good.

STAY IN TOUCH

Managers and other leaders change in any organization. If you have a good contact with someone in an organization that supports your emergency plan, make sure you mark on your calendar dates to reach out and touch base with them during the year. Then if there has been a change, you can ask to meet with them and give the new person some background on how they have helped your school by being part of the school's emergency plan. Again, we may not need to use the resource but far better for them to be prepared and not needed than it is for them to be needed and not prepared!

Keep your contact numbers handy! Whether you make a small card to keep taped to your radio or in your wallet or a laminated sheet in your incident command box, you should have those contact numbers handy all day. Then you can make the call easily without waiting to find the right number to call. Even having contact numbers available to you in the evening may not be a bad idea; you may have some concerns about a natural weather issue or possible mechanical problem that you reach out to see if they have any large parties the next day. Then if you do indeed need them, you are already in the know!

Also remember to keep your district office in the loop. Usually it is frowned upon for a principal to sign a contract or a memorandum of understanding (a contract that lays out what the organization can do for the school during an emergency.) If you think strategically, if each principal had his or her own deals in place with different vendors and a district has hundreds of school, it would be a nightmare to manage. Instead, work with your district to find places that may be able to work with multiple schools.

LESSONS LEARNED

- There are agencies other than public safety that can help out during an emergency.
- Public works staff are usually municipal workers who are great at handling emergencies and have a lot of special equipment.
- Food trucks are a great and portable way to supply food during an incident.
- Porta potties may be a necessity during a prolonged issue.

- Private bus contractors can supply air-conditioned and comfortable buses with lavatory facilities to accommodate workers during breaks or in staging.
- Look for nontraditional places to accommodate your needs during an evacuation such as churches or hotels with banquet facilities.
- Make sure you have good agreements with outside suppliers and keep in contact with them.

Chapter 11

Communications

One of the most overlooked yet important aspects of incident command is communication. Often the difference between a successful incident response and a difficult or even failed response rests with your ability to effectively communicate. Every aspect of the process involves communication, and it is well worth the effort to preplan how your team will address those communications.

There are often two types of communications that we should focus our efforts on, internal communications and external communications. Internal communications involve ways that we share information with the personnel within our school. There are three types of internal stakeholders that we address internally: ICS team members, staff members, and students. Each of those groups has a different perspective and reception base, so it is important to look at how you craft your message to each internal group.

INTERNAL COMMUNICATIONS

Start with your team. These folks are the key to how you effectively manage an incident. You have to trust them to help you make critical decisions. What does it take to make a critical decision? Information and the authority to get information. If your planning chiefs needs to know how many students are in school today, they should not have to ask you to check with your secretary. The secretary should know who is on the team and that they have access to whatever information they need during an incident. Make that clear to everyone in the school that your team is an extension of you. That distinction creates two very helpful results in perception. First, it clears up questions about roles before an incident actually occurs. Second it shows your team that you are supportive of their role in keeping students safe as part of your ICS team. Both are good messages to get out.

Now staff communications. There are multiple trains of thought on this and you should find one that works for you. Some believe that communications should be limited to staff in order to avoid distraction and allow them to continue their work teaching in the classroom. Anyone who has ever spent time as a classroom teacher knows full well what occurs during a lockdown or crisis. *Teachers don't teach, they text!*

We live in a news and access-driven society. We are used to hearing about breaking news and getting firsthand reports from news media sources that operate online and on screen twenty-four hours per day. These are usually distant events that don't even have a local impact. Now what about an event that is occurring outside their classroom door? They won't be able to check CNN or the web for hints as to what's going on and that bothers them! After all, if we can find out about a bombing in Egypt seconds after it happens, why can't we find out about an intruder in our own building within seconds?

So perhaps meeting in the middle would be best. Designate a communications person to handle those internal stakeholders. If you lockdown due to a police activity down the street, there is nothing wrong with having someone send a quick email to staff alerting them to the situation outside. If they are aware of the reality, they will not fall prey to the literally hundreds of possibilities which their imagination will bring to the table!

The internal communications channel also helps as you develop your incident action plan. If you are planning to evacuate the school to another location, prepare the staff for this possibility. Give them the time to gather what they will need such as class rosters and their personal belongings. While teachers will do what you expect them to do just as you instruct, if you give them the courtesy of a heads-up and include them in your process, they become yet another extended part of your team. They will appreciate it, and you will find that your team will be more effective because of the high level of communication.

As a mental note to help develop your internal communications, always use the word BID to help you craft your message. BID stands for background, information, and direction. For the background just in a sentence or two tell the staff what created the situation, if you know what it is. Don't just tell them what is currently going on because they will ask why it happened; if you know, briefly explain it. Next is information, a chance to give them information on the current status of the school and the incident. That can include what outside agencies such as public works or the fire department are coming to help.

Let's apply the concept in practice. You are a principal in an elementary school in an urban community. Your office receives a call from the local police dispatcher that they are sending officers to a house several blocks away for a barricaded person. They want you to lockdown your school. You order the external lockdown and notify your district office. Now it's time to communicate with the staff. You may draft a BID message like this:

> A few minutes ago we were contacted by the local police who are handling an incident several blocks away involving a barricaded person. As a safety precaution we are going into an external lockdown and keeping students in from outside recess. We will not change our operations internally. Just go through the normal indoor recess procedures. I will contact you after the issue is resolved or if we receive further information from their officers. Thank you for your support in keeping the school day going as usual during this event.

Now you can make a simple PA announcement asking teachers to check their email for a message about a change in the schedule for the day. This would not sound alarming to students but would ensure that teachers know to check their email for the message.

The last internal stakeholder is the student body. How we communicate with them is really a key factor in how we accomplish our primary goals of keeping accountability of the students and keeping them safe. Panic usually does not lend itself to safety. Neither does fear. So you must decide what information they need to know in order to prepare for whatever tasks may be necessary for them. Start by asking yourself about your students!

Obviously in an elementary school you would have the limited ability to effectively share information about an incident with students. However, these students also need more comfort, support, and confidence in their caretakers than average high school students. So the shift goes from the amount of information to the way positive and supportive communication is handled. Students need to be reassured that although something "different" is going on, they are safe and will continue to remain safe. This message should come from you as the principal as well as the teachers in the classroom.

Middle-school students pose a different challenge. Some are mature enough to handle a role in their own self-preservation with little support or guidance. Others need positive reinforcement as well as more directed guidance and set expectations. If you are evacuating to buses for a transfer to another school, explain how the shift will occur, not necessarily why. Just provide the direction and leave them with the affirmation that everything is fine, and they are being moved as a safety precaution. Usually this will be enough to quell any fears about what is going on and allow them to act as if this were just another routine school event.

High school students offer yet another complexity. These students are social media and information savvy, so in the absence of information they will do whatever they can to find it. You will need to provide direction as well as a brief description of what the incident is. These students typically need more of a "why" they are doing something than just a what. They question authority, and it will ultimately benefit you if you provide at least the basic information. It will reduce confusion as well as increase cooperation by the students. Both are important if you have a complicated incident.

EXTERNAL STAKEHOLDERS

Externally there are also three different types of external stakeholders: district leadership, parents, and the general public. Just as we said before about our internal stakeholders, your external stakeholders have three different perspectives and your messages should be crafted to meet each of their needs.

Your district office will be asking what they need to do in order to support your school during an incident. Do not be shy! Ask for whatever you may need to support you. Sometimes a few extra hands go a long way during a crisis. Also a good time to ask for your district spokesperson to come out to the school if you anticipate that the press may become aware of an issue at your school. Take that off your own plate by getting the professional public information officer to come help!

Parents are the next big priority. These folks are worried about their children. It is imperative that you communicate with parents quickly and effectively. Use empathy to think about what you would want to know if you were a parent. Just as we said with your teaching staff, an absence of information would lead to the nightmare scenario for parents who would unleash their imagination. There is a caveat, however. Remember your priorities are always the accountability and safety of students. Communicate with parents only after you have established the student safety and a path forward to ensure their continued safety.

The other consideration for the parent communication is what it will contain. A vague information update will cause more confusion and may send the parents flooding into your incident scene before you are ready for them. Just as we would do with high school students, we need to communicate the basic background of the incident as well as provide some direction for what parents should expect and what you expect of parents. If the campus is closed, announce that. Let them know when you expect they can reunite with their kids if there will be an early dismissal or relocation. The more you communicate with the parents, the less phone calls your office staff will get asking for clarification.

This is a good time to review one of the basic concepts of communications and that is called the communications channel. When you look at this theory, a message originates with the sender who crafts the message with a certain intent and understanding. Next there is the noise that is created when the message is transmitted. This noise can be anything from the method of communication or editing of the message or even translation into foreign languages. Whatever it is, it changes the basis for our message. Then you have the recipient's state of mind and experience level when they receive it. They are listening with a certain filter and depending on how much noise changed your message. They could receive something entirely different.

Remember the old telephone game where you sit in a circle and you start by whispering something to the person next to you who then whispers the same message to the person next to them all the way around the room. What happens when you hear the message back? You all laugh because it is nowhere close to what you originally said. Well add the intensity of communications being impacted by an emergency, and the level of miscommunication skyrockets.

Now you can begin looking at how external communications should work. In the modern age of every student (from kindergarten on up) has a cell phone, they will actively text their parents and friends so that messages (right or wrong) will be going out to many of the folks connected to your school. Some students will ask their parents to come pick them up while some parents will decide independently that they need to come to make sure that their "babies" are safe. This adds some complication to your accountability process. Also if you have not established your release team, then mistakes can happen and students may be released to the wrong parent or worse, a person who is not a parent.

One thing you definitely want to avoid is parents being informed of an issue by the media before hearing about it from you. This would create an immense amount of confusion as well as breed distrust. Parents trust that we will keep them in the loop well before the local television station would! Remember that parents are worried about their children and their intentions are not to interfere with your incident command but to take care of their most important person in their lives, even if you send a quick instant message to parents that informs them of the nature of the incident and reassures them that their children are safe and that the incident is being managed. If you do not want them to come directly to the school, ask them to be patient and wait for further instructions. This can be important if your response includes relocating students to another school for dismissal. It would complicate operations to have parents appear when you are trying to get students onto buses and when responders are trying to deal with whatever emergency is occurring.

What about when the crisis involves the entire community? Even if there is a major natural disaster, parents primary concern will be for the welfare of their children. While the media coverage may discuss the entire area, you will need to ensure that you are sending out targeted communications directed toward parents. If homes are impacted, you may consider working with your district to reunite families with their students at the school. Most schools may also serve as emergency shelters, so it would make sense to bring families in rather than sending students home into what could be a high risk environment.

If the police or fire department has a PIO, it is usually a good idea to let them talk. After all, they are usually handling a majority of the emergency aspects of your incident. Usually in schools our comments are not directed toward what caused the issue or how much damage there could be; we usually explain the status of those students in our care and how parents can be reunited or reassured as to their children's well-being. Either the police or fire PIO can pass along those messages as well, again allowing you to focus on making sure that your students are indeed safe and secure.

COMMUNICATIONS DISCIPLINE

Everyone will be reaching out during an emergency to find out what is going on and how they are impacted. As the incident commander, your focus should remain on your mission, managing the incident at hand. Only communicate with the ICS team for now; let your cell phone ring! Better yet, hand it off to a staffer who does not have responsibility. It takes discipline not to answer every cell phone call but that usually has a few negative consequences. First it distracts from your current train of thought and where you are with your team. Usually it is someone adding to your concerns and creating some form of confusion. Now is the time for you to focus! Whoever called will understand when you say that you were being briefed or working with your ICS team to manage an emergency and didn't have time to talk.

Radio discipline is another area that requires some effort. Sometimes when we give someone a portable radio, he or she tends to become a disc jockey and want to use the radio as his or her own microphone to the world! Put a stop to that. Let staff members with radios know that they should only communicate important and relevant information and should keep off the radio as much as possible. There are several reasons for this. First, we don't know who is listening! If teachers or the office has radios and parents or students are around, they can listen to the radio if someone is screaming or crying or cursing or delivering a lengthy and detailed description of what horrible event is befalling a fellow student or staff member. That is not good and only adds to the confusion.

The next reason is simply a matter of safety. If you have people operating in an unsafe environment and they become injured or discover something important, they need to be able to communicate that information now. If someone else is tying up the radio with unimportant updates and taking a long time, it keeps the rest of you from hearing the calls for help. This is even more important during the regular school day. Don't tie up the radio with foolish comments or useless information. That may keep the nurse from calling about a real emergency, or another staff member who becomes involved with a significant fight would be unable to call for back up.

Keeping off the radio for you as the incident commander also allows you to focus and for others to see you as evaluating and giving the orders that need to be given. We will talk about command mind-set in a later chapter but for now remember that your staff, students, and parents depend on you to be the calm face for them. Yell and scream in the radio and the last thing you sound like is a confident person who is in control. Measure your words and the way that you say them *before* you open the mic and begin to speak whether you are on the walkie talkie or on the PA.

There was an old fire chief who used to stand in front of fire scenes with an unlit cigar in his mouth. When asked why he always chewed on a cigar at fires, he said that it forced him to think before he spoke, he had to take the cigar out of his mouth to give commands and therefore could focus on making good decisions and communicating them effectively. Now most schools are tobacco-free so you may not be able to chew on a cigar but keep the thought in mind; think before you speak so that your communications are crisp and well thought-out. In addition, you need to think about the importance of honest communication with key team members.

In situations where a staff member may have suffered from a medical issue or been injured, this is an important step because as you all know, schools are close communities. A colleague in trouble will lead the staff to worry about their fallen friends and not focus on the jobs at hand. Reassure them that the staff member is being cared for to ease their fears and concerns. These radio calls require your immediate attention and will require you to quickly make sure someone is taking care of the staff member *and* remind the rest of the staff that they still have a responsibility for the safety of their students.

LESSONS LEARNED

- Effective communication is often the key to an efficient incident response.
- Staff members *need* to be informed about what is occurring.
- Consideration should be given to how much information parents need to receive and when they should receive it.
- Parents should *never* find out about an incident from the mass media.

Section IV

RECOVERY

Chapter 12

Recovery Phase

So the emergency is finished. The fire trucks and police cars are gone, and the parents and their children are at home. The emergency is over right? Wrong! In fact, the last phase of the cycle can very well be the longest and most tedious. Recovery is the act of returning everything in the school to normalcy (or as close as we can get to "normal" in schools!). That encompasses many different moving parts and requires almost as much effort as the response to the emergency itself!

There are several different types of things that must be strategically addressed. Some are obvious, and some will require some thought. Obvious things include physical repairs. If there was a pipe burst, there will be remediation and reconstruction of damaged physical spaces as well as repair of the pipe itself. Classroom supplies or files may need to be replaced, and certainly any supplies used to respond to the incident need to be replaced so that learning can continue.

Next come those more intangible items such as the mental well-being of the students. Certainly there are events such as school shootings or the death of a student (on or off campus) that have a lasting psychological impact on any student. Remember we discussed before that an "incident" is anything that interferes with our students' ability to learn? Certainly the grieving process is one of those situations. If a high school student his or her life from a car accident, it may take a month before the students begin to truly recover mentally and return to normal school operation.

Just as you needed the guidance of trained emergency responders to manage your incident or emergency, often you will need experts here as well. Helping to figure out what students' body need to support them through grieving or mental recovery from an incident really depends on the nature of the student body, how tight-knit they are, how their relationship is with your staff. All of these have an impact on how you begin to recover from whatever you have suffered.

There are always two different views that seem to be expressed regarding the amount of support that a school provides during the recovery process. Some say, students should be returned to their "routine" as quickly as possible to get their minds off whatever occurred. Others believe that the school is a great place to bring resources together in a strong supportive environment where you are surrounded by a strong support system of your peers. Again, this is a local decision based on you and your team. In some cases your school may not have the tools to provide adequate support in which case a more community-based recovery plan should be used.

There are also going to be times when you did not suffer an emergency at all yet your resources will be needed to create a recovery operation for something that you didn't even respond too. One example that stands out for all of us is September 11, 2001. Your school may have not been directly impacted but certainly we all had to provide some sort of mental health support for our students. Even in California, students felt the crushing emotion of what was occurring in New York. These students were certainly not going to focus on instruction, nor were their teachers. You have a duty to respond during these times and provide the same services you would provide if the event happened in your own backyard.

So what does that response look like? Did your school district have a team of crisis professionals that will come out to your school to assist after an emergency? Perhaps your school psychologist or school counselor has a training in what is called critical incident stress management? This is a system developed by emergency response personnel to help deal with stress after emergencies. There are absolutely resources in your state and local fire service to help.

We should also look at incidents where there will never be a clear-cut "end" or recovery. Instances include a school shooting that occurs in your school. Regardless of what mental health support or recovery efforts you have in place, there will never be a time when your school is completely back to normal. In these situations, we need to define what the "new normal" will be. There are times when our entire culture has changed and we must acknowledge that as part of the recovery process.

New York City a few years after the September 11 attacks experienced this type of new normal. Commuters were used to see NYPD officers armed with assault rifles in their subway systems and having their bags checked each time they traveled. This would have been out of the ordinary before the attacks, but the city became used to this as the norm. The same can be said of schools. There is eventually a time after a deep-seated crisis occurs in your school that you have to draw the line and say, it is what it is and try to go on teaching. We all hope that you never experience a tragedy like that during your time in schools, but best to be prepared for it.

Another important aspect of the recovery process is your staff and their mental health. While the focus is (and should be) on helping the children that we serve and their mental health, we cannot forget about those who provide it. A large part of the critical incident stress management process came about because of the lasting mental health impacts on first responders after witnessing so many emergencies. Your staff will need similar help. They may witness students that they have watched grow and cared for being hurt or suffering during the emergency; they may not admit it but they will need some help.

One good habit to establish after an emergency is the debriefing process. There are two parts to the system that will benefit you, your emergency team and your school staff. First is the incident wrap-up critique. This is when all of the team, including staff, gets together to discuss what went well during the operation and what needs to be improved upon before another incident occurs. Usually it should happen soon after the event is over, but after everyone has had a chance to recover from the adrenalin rush and post adrenaline fall that always occurs after every emergency. The next morning or afternoon is fine. This should be focused on positive critiques of the system. Staff should avoid saying things like, "Tom didn't get the information on where students were being staged to Operations quickly." It would be better to say, "we should look at ways to reduce the amount of time it takes for information to get to the operations branch chief." Look at the system and not the individual who assumed each role.

Another fantastic resource when you're looking at students includes reviewing whether or not students saw things that could be improved for their safety. It's as important to include students as it is some staff in your planning process. The students have a sense of ownership in their school and should be included in decisions that impact their safety. Remember we may do this every day, but they have a fresh perspective on some of the issues that are facing the school. They can be a real benefit in this process.

A few days after the event should be your staff's mental health debrief. The purpose is for the team to discuss how they feel and how they support each other. It is good for people to understand that they might not be the only ones who can't sleep a few days after an incident and that it is normal. The focus here is to not talk about the incident itself but rather how everyone is dealing with the stress afterward. Usually one of your counsellors can lead the session, but it is important for you as the leader to acknowledge that this is a useful process and that it is important to discuss.

The last important aspect of recovery is to make sure that all of the paperwork, equipment, and supplies used during the response is resupplied, restored, and put in place so that your team can respond effectively the next time. The ambulance crew on an ambulance clean up and resupply at the hospital so that they can be ready if someone calls for help while they return to the station; your team should think the same way. Make sure the oxygen that the nurse used gets refilled, or the forms in your incident command packet get replaced if you use them. Radios get recharged and placed where they can be used next time.

This is not the end of the loop realistically. This is when you take those pieces of information from the debriefing process and use the lessons learned to begin in the planning phase again. You now can add an event to your risk assessment. You can look at the tools that you had available and determine if you need to change the way your plan addresses different aspects of the incident or even make a list of items that you need to address in the mitigation phase after you have made any changes in the plan.

Make sure if you make any substantive plan changes, your entire team is aware of them and change their copies of the document. Remember we said that it is a living document. It should change because we constantly learn things and experience different aspects of incident response which can impact our plan. We may even read about a response or an incident in a trade publication and decide that you should follow their best practices or include something else in your plan. This is a good thing. The plan shouldn't be stagnant but the more you revisit it, the better your team will be at implementing the document and the system when you need to.

LESSONS LEARNED

- Just because the emergency part of the incident is over does not mean that there is still not work to be done!
- After the incident our primary focus is always on the physical and mental well-being of the students. They may need time and resources to process what they have experienced.
- The ICS team should evaluate what worked and ways to improve how they manage such incidents in the future.
- All of the staff should debrief and discuss the emotional toll that some incidents take on the staff, not just the students.
- Equipment should be recharged, replaced, and readied for the next incident.

Section V

MITIGATION AND PREPAREDNESS PHASES AGAIN

Chapter 13

Training for Game Day

Welcome back, commander! We have reviewed all of the roles and responsibilities that you will have as an incident commander in your school as well as how to effectively manage your team. Now you are probably looking forward to a challenging tabletop exercise that will force you and your team to use all of your newfound skills and test your abilities to the fullest. Let's jump right into your exercise and planning for a . . . wait for it . . . graduation!

A GREAT WAY TO PRACTICE WITH ICS—USE IT!

There is usually a brief look of confusion on school teams' faces when they are told that their first exercise is not responding to a horrific disaster at school but the sublime planning for a graduation. Remember that the system is not called "emergency command system" but rather "ICS." In chapter 1, we discussed the difference between an incident and an emergency. The system works just as well for both. In fact, the secret service as well as most major public safety organizations use this tool to plan for events such as Inauguration Day.

This is a great way to keep your staff familiar with ICS as well as allows you to use a time-tested and effective ready-made organizational tool to help prepare for such events. Once you try using ICS for planning non-emergency events, you will likely keep returning and never go back to the old way. In fact, everyone who has ever planned a wedding knows the intricacies and the amount of elements that must come together on the big day. There was a couple in Pennsylvania who used the system to plan their big day! They were both officers in the fire service, but they used it to effectively manage the out-of-control event known as their wedding day!

In figure 13.1, you can see some suggested uses for the system when preparing for the graduation. It is always good to start with the organization chart as that is the heart of ICS and will help get the team members acclimated to their roles as they progress through the scenario. Start with who is in charge. The incident commander may not be the principal for this event; if there is a faculty member who has been running graduation for years, that person could assume the role. The only rule about who is the best to serve as incident commander is that it is someone who has the legal right to assume the role as well as the experience.

Next, look at your branches. Operations for a graduation include things such as bringing in the flow of guests and directing the students to their assembly points and preparing them to enter the facility. Graduations typically include security, so another section under operations will be security. This is often provided by the venue, but your operations section chief will need to coordinate their efforts. Seating for the students and invited VIPs also falls under the operations team.

Planning for this event will include areas such as planning for parking areas and where the flow of traffic will allow students to be dropped off prior to the event. How many brochures will be needed and where will they be located for guests to pick up? Creating maps of the venue (including emergency egress routes for VIPS and students) is also a job for the planning branch. Keeping things on schedule is the biggest job for planning. Also unlike an emergency where accountability is part of operations, in this scenario planning will be the key because they need to know how many students are graduating in order to create the seating charts and programs.

Logistics is another key aspect for a graduation. Does the venue have a radio system, and can your team get portable radios to allow for

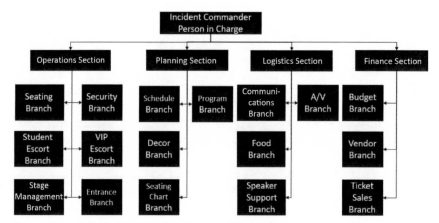

Figure 13.1. Sample Organization Chart for Graduation

communication between your ICS team and the venue security and operations team? Communications is often an issue when an event rolls around, but using ICS the logistics section chiefs will know that they are responsible and will have a decent cell phone contact list as well as any other necessary communications. Is there a luncheon or snacks for the invited dignitaries and speakers? Logistics should prepare in advance for ensuring that any refreshments are ready.

Is this an outdoor event during a hot day? Logistics would look at having water stations located in the area for guests and students. Planning will look at things such as medical emergencies; is there an ambulance on stand-by and if not, who will be responsible to call if an emergency arises? Remember the goal of having the planning section involved in the ICS at all is to think about what could possibly occur and make a contingency plan for it. Then if something occurs during the event, there is no need to think, just simply react according to what you already planned! If nothing goes awry, then you have had a successful event and can feel great that you were prepared for anything!

Remember we said before that you may not need a finance section during most emergencies? Well you certainly will need one for graduation! Someone needs to be responsible for collecting receipts for flowers from the floral company for guests. Who is paying for the programs? Finance will also keep track of what funds came in from any ticket sales (if you sell tickets) or any donated revenue that is used. Again this is a great way to distribute responsibilities so that items such as these are not afterthoughts or assigned as they come up. If you thought through the responsibilities and developed a reasonable organization chart, half of the organization tasks are complete well before the event.

Next we look at setting up the operational priorities and timeline, that is, determining what is important and who is assigned to make it happen when. In our graduation scenario, the planning section chief may be assigned to work with the venue to determine when it is available for the ceremony and discuss how many people it will hold. Meanwhile the finance section can begin developing the budget and determining where funds can be raised and how they can be spent to support the operations. Logistics can work with the principal to see who the guests will be and how they will be supported. Usually all of the teams should attend at least one walk-through before planning the event so that they have a good idea of what they are actually planning for.

Here is another key ICS tip: do not reinvent the wheel! Most venues have security and operational employees who have worked these events in the past. Rather than developing your own plan for where students enter and where programs are distributed, just ask your hosts! Their parking plan is usually best and will save you tons of time and wasted planning efforts. (Remember the same applies to real emergencies, the fire department has personnel who are seasoned emergency leaders and can be a huge help with your team as you manage an incident, just ask!)

Once each section chief has finished his or her part of the plan, get together for a briefing. Each section chief should brief the rest of the team on his or her portion of the master incident plan. This should include timelines and who will actually perform what duties on the day of the event. This is also a great time to have someone sit in from the venue who can add support. In the weeks prior to a presidential visit anywhere in the country, there is a meeting just like this where all of the plans are run through to see what is missing and how the event can be run smoothly. A team can work together to see where there needs improvement far better than one person struggling on game day!

Once the plan is briefed and approved by the team and the incident command, put it all on paper and distribute it to the team. Include things like key cellular phone contacts and radio channels to be used on the day of the event including who is assigned a radio. This becomes the script for the event, and everyone should have a copy so that everyone on the team is aware of what the key issues are and when they are addressed. This finished product is called an incident action plan and should be used every time your team is used (if time permits a formal process, if not informal is fine.)

On graduation day, you will find that things run far smother than they ever have before! Because you shared responsibility, there is shared command and control and a distribution of leadership. People will take pride in ensuring that their branch does its job well. There will be hiccups (such as a real emergency in the middle of the event), but if everyone has the same mind-set, the program will continue to run as planned while the team does what it needs to do for the emergency. The team has prepared for the event; each has run through it several times, and now they are literally just doing what comes naturally after their early effort.

After the event, bring the team back together for a debrief. This is where your team discusses what went right, what went wrong, and what could be done better next time. This is often an overlooked step in the response process, but it is an important step. Benjamin Franklin said that "the definition of insanity is doing the same thing in the same way over and over again yet expecting a different result." If we make the same mistake over and over again, we will never learn and improve.

The debriefing should also be written down and included with a copy of the IAP and saved for the team to use later for training or review. Team members should be honest and constructive in finding ways to improve the way the team functioned during the training exercise or the event. This way they will continue to gel into an effective emergency management tool. Football teams strive to practice plays and create unity long before they ever hit the field against an opponent. Our ICS team is no different. The day to learn all the plays and what position you are playing is *not* on game day.

This same mentality should be used by the team to prepare for their more important role during actual emergencies. At least once a month the team should get together to talk about potential issues in the coming month and to take time to assume their ICS roles as a refresher. If winter months are rolling in and your community suffers from extreme ice exposure, discuss how you would respond to an ice event if it occurred during the school day. What would each member of the team have to address in their part of the ICS to effectively and safely get students home from either an early dismissal or a regular end of the day under hazardous weather conditions?

There is an old saying in the military that says "sweat spilled in training prevents blood being spilled in battle." While it seems grotesque, it is right on target. Team members should always think and train as if they were managing a real emergency with real lives and student safety on the line. It can be said that the most precious thing that parents give us is the gift of caring for their child during the school day. They may forgive us if we do not teach their child everything as long as we do not let them fall into harm's way while in our care. At the end of the day, ICS is about protecting lives.

But I am an elementary school principal? Do I plan fifth-grade graduation?

Well, you certainly can use it for fifth-grade move-up, but you also have a lot more opportunities to use the system than most secondary school principals and can use it to actually have a real impact on student safety during a time when you have the least control over student safety! What is the most dangerous event that most elementary school students regularly encounter? While some of you may say dodgeball (if you are still even allowed to play it) or recess, there is one other major threat to student safety.

At least half of our readers are jumping in their seats and yelling at the book that the answer is "field trips!" Congratulations, you get a smiley face! Anyone who has been in elementary school teaching for more than five years can usually share a story of some horrible field trip where they lost a student or someone got hurt and what a nightmare it was. After all, we can control the safety of students for the most part when they are in school because we can control who has access to them as well as the things that surround them. When on a field trip we are at the mercy of the elements as well as the safety procedures for whatever venue we are visiting as well as the nature of the other visitors at that venue. One good rule of thumb for ICS is the less control you have over the safety of your students, the more planning and effort that is required to keep them safe! What a great time to use ICS!

So as we did in the graduation example, let's look at the basic organization structure then to see how each of those branches may function. In figure 13.2 you can see a basic overview of the organization chart (hopefully you are getting used to those by now and will start using them!)

Who will the incident commander be? That depends on who will be on the trip and who will be in charge when they are on the trip. While normally for in-school incidents, the IC is the principal or the assistant principal; in this case usually they are not on the trip itself so they wouldn't be in charge. This is usually a good role for the lead teacher or senior teacher on the trip. If the English department is going, who is the head of the department? Other teachers are used to them being a resource when they have teaching questions so it would not be unusual for them to be comfortable looking to that staff member for leadership during an emergency.

The other branches really just depend on who is comfortable doing them during planning. The operations branch will not have a ton to do during the planning phase but will be used a ton on the day of the trip. They will be the one on the trip who maintains the phone list or radios that the planning chief sets up for use to communicate. Operations will ensure accountability before the buses leave, after they arrive at the destination, and once again when they load for the return trip and get back for release to parents or at school. Operations will be important if someone gets hurt or lost, and they will have to muster the resources needed to find the student or care for the one who was hurt.

Planning and logistics will work together for most of the pre-trip preparation. Planning will work on things like where the students go for trip, making the contact and getting the contracts for the venue to the principal for approvals.

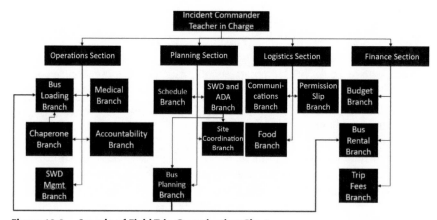

Figure 13.2.   Sample of Field Trip Organization Chart

PUTTING IT ALL TOGETHER

Having practiced for a graduation, now let's look at how you would possibly handle a real emergency, such as smoke in the school. It is just another day at your school when a staff member coming from the faculty lounge notices what seems like the smell of smoke down one of the school's hallways. He or she has to do something, but what?

The first few steps in the response phase are the most important. The first person to discover the emergency can be the difference between success or failure in the effective management of the emergency. That is why every staff member should believe that he or she is a key member of the team and may well be the first person on the scene of an emergency and the one that initiates the ICS.

Remember your size-up, the method of looking at the nature of the emergency and determining how many resources you may need to effectively manage the incident and what those resources may be. One major rule of thumb here is to think about having more resources available to assist you than having less. During the size-up phase of response, be liberal about asking for help. It is far better to have help show up and tell them that you don't need their services than not to have the help and skilled professionals that you need when you need them. When in doubt, call the fire department for help! They are the experts, and nothing that you receive in this text can replace their professional experience at handling emergencies; it can just help you to effectively manage your end of the emergency.

(Remember the "know where the kids are and that they are safe"?) So if you see smoke, do not wait to see if you can find the source of the fire; your size-up ends in the fact that there is smoke which usually means there is fire and *that* poses a risk to your students and staff safety! You now know that you have to act.

You begin by pulling the fire alarm. This is probably the easiest method for notifying the fire department of a problem, getting the students out of the building, and getting your ICS team moving. You make your way out to the designated command post (the back of your Chevy Tahoe since it is roomy enough), and your secretary brings out the bag that has your command post stuff in it. You put on your incident commander vest and begin using the white board to note the time that you smelled the smoke and where on your floor plan the smoke seems to be coming from.

Your planning and logistics section chiefs are right behind you already listening for the accountability reports to make sure that everyone is out of the building; the operations section chief is making sure that the search of the building for anyone that remains inside is taken care of. Next your planning chief begins thinking about where fire trucks may need to be staged because this is a real fire so there may be a lot more than just a few. He recommends that you move the students from the front of the school to the side so that they will not be in the way of the fire apparatus in case you are there for a while. You agree and assign the operations team to assist with those once they are finished searching.

The fire chief pulls up and walks to your command post for a briefing on what is going on. After you describe what you see, he begins to use his ICS to address their issues, such as searching the school again and finding the fire. You inform him that everyone is accounted for and that the students are being maintained away from the staging area so that he doesn't have to worry about them. As a precaution he sends his ambulance to where your nurse has set up to form the medical team that will address any medical issues that occur.

As the fire department searches for the cause of the smoke, your planning and logistics chiefs are looking at the "what's next?" How long will it be, and will they have to move the students? How many students are here today? Your logistics person can now be looking at how many students are present and how many buses would be required to house them all. The person can also begin thinking about meals and restrooms. If we are going to be a while, we may need to feed students and will certainly need to find a place for them to go to the bathroom.

The incident commander from the school and fire department should be discussing whether it is best to initiate a dismissal or send the students to an off campus site to await either release from school or a return to the campus. This is a key question because if it is going to be a long effort, the presence of so many students may hinder the fire department's ability to do their job. In reality it may also be easier to provide for an organized dismissal from a site that is not already clogged with emergency responders and equipment.

Now the ICS is working like a well-oiled machine; all of the moving parts are focused on what they are supposed to be managing so that no one person bears the brunt of the decision-making process. It makes it easier to look for solutions and pros and cons if it is done by a team of professionals rather than one sole leader.

Remember that other tool in your ICS toolbox, the "OODA Loop?" This is a good time to apply the loop again as you look at this new scenario. The OODA stands for Observe, Orient, Decide, and Act. Let's look again at each step.

First *observe*. This is where you look at what the circumstances are pre-senting you right now. In the preceding example, the students are evacuated and sitting on buses, and the fire department may tell you that they haven't found the source of the smoke. Those are two key observations at this stage.

Next we *orient* ourselves, that is, put what we know into context quickly. The students have been out for an hour and a half, and some will start becoming concerned and may begin needing added resources such as their medication or food and restroom facilities. You cannot orient yourself to the fire department aspect because they have yet to find the source of the smoke.

Now it is time for a decision. Looking at both of these factors you may decide that it is time to get the students to a different location that can temporarily support their needs and allow you to organize for a dismissal if necessary. Your ICS team should meet and see if everyone agrees that this is the best move. Remember to consult the IC (incident commander) from the fire department as well. They may be able to provide some guidance as far as the length of their operation as you discuss the logistics of your moves.

Finally, the last step is to *act*. This is where we put our decision into effect. You may find out that the auditorium at the high school a mile away can safely accommodate all of your students. This is a perfect place to get the students and be able to keep them secure and provide them with services while you either wait for the resolution at your school or the decision to dismiss.

What happens next? You start at observe all over again. Now the buses are on their way. You start asking questions of your ICS team. How are we maintaining accountability as we bring students into the auditorium? Are we working with our host school to find facilities that can be dedicated to our students and keep them segregated from the host high school students? Is there a place where our nurse can set up shop so that she can begin meeting the needs of our students? All of these observations should begin before your buses ever get to the other school.

You will continue using the loop as a guide to your process all the way until the incident is controlled and all of the students are safely with their parents or back in their classrooms.

Once at the new site, your ICS team can start planning for the next steps. If your contact at your school tells you that it may be hours, you may begin considering an early dismissal from your new location. Most districts have a policy regarding who can order an early dismissal and how that can be communicated. That should all be incorporated in your plan and in your current planning process.

Your planning team will need to work on how the dismissal will be organized. There are only three ways that our students leave school normally: by bus, by car, and on foot. A plan needs to be created for how each will be managed. Between your planning and logistics person you should assess what facilities are in place at the host school to accommodate your dismissal. Is there room for car line and buses at the same time, or should you have the buses pick up their students first then ask the car line to come after the buses have left? What about your walkers? Perhaps they lived within a block of your home school but now you are miles away from your school at the new host school? Do you have a bus lined up to bring walkers home or will you contact their parents to have them join car line and pick them up?

Once again the glory of ICS is that this is all being planned by a team and not just a single person. Each team member is focused on his or her area of responsibility and that makes sure that balls aren't left in the air. Questions get answered and solutions found far easier when a team problem solves.

This scenario occurs almost every day at schools around the world. There is usually gnashing of teeth and frustrated sighs as school leaders bump into issues after issue because they did not have an organized ICS in place, and the time to build your ICS team is not on the day of the disaster.

Because you have more tools and training, your ICS team managed the incident rather than the incident managing you. Students were dismissed in an orderly fashion from the off-site high school, and the fire department discovered an electrical fire in a light ballast in a storage room. It was quickly extinguished, and they have been working with your maintenance staff to ensure that school will be ready in the morning.

You can feel proud of the job that your team did because you followed the *Guiding Rule of School Incident Command*; you always knew where the students were and that they were safe. Your job here is done! Nice job IC! (Now get ready for your *next* emergency!)

DRILLS AND INTERNAL EXERCISES

It is important for your entire school to practice the plan during regular fire drills. Make sure that you are testing the system, and try a different alarm pull station each time. Do not always plan drills for certain times, like regular class times. Have you practiced toward the end of a lunch? Do the students know where they will go if there is a fire during lunch? Emergencies do not happen on a certain schedule, so plan for them to happen at the worst possible time.

Block off intersections so that teachers have to think quickly about alternate routes of egress. Do not inform them each time there is a drill; part of emergency management is being prepared all the time, not just when an emergency is scheduled. If your staff responds in the same way all of the time, they don't need to worry about whether it is a real emergency or not; they will always do the right thing.

EXERCISE YOUR PLAN, TOO

One of the biggest questions that most new ICS practitioners ask is "what is the difference between an exercise and a drill?" Great question! The difference is that a drill is an internal practice session, while an exercise usually involves several agencies, hopefully the same ones that will respond during an actual emergency. That includes the local fire department, police department, emergency medical services, and emergency management agency.

The exercise cycle usually starts with a tabletop, which allows all of the participants to get to know each other and how they might function during an event. Once everyone is familiar, they can begin planning for a fully functional exercise. This will involve actually deploying resources in real time, just as they would occur during an emergency. Start with your local emergency management agency, which always has a staff that is trained and ready to assist with exercise planning. It can help look at your plan and the agencies that work with your school to develop a successful planning roadmap to get your exercise on the way.

The bottom line goal of an exercise is to have everyone practice how they would handle a true emergency. If the fire department assumes their roles in the ICS and your team assumes their roles in ICS, then you will in real time be able to practice unified command (remember that from ICS, that is when two or more separate ICS teams from different agencies work together as one combined incident command team?) It is good practice for everyone.

Don't discount the networking opportunity either! We always have retreats or conventions where we get together with colleagues and discuss our schools and how we do our jobs, but we rarely get to sit down with the folks that will help us during an emergency. A full-scale exercise is a great way to meet the key players in the agencies that support and protect your school. Exchange business cards and begin developing a relationship so you are not meeting them for the first time during a disaster!

Now let's have a brief look at a few scenarios that you will most assuredly encounter at least once during your tenure as a building administrator (and incident commander). One of the most intimidating can be the bomb threat, which is fortunately a rare event but when it happens, it can cause great consternation and fear. However, we can break it down and make it a manageable event that can assure that your students are safe.

First, this is one of those events that you know you are not alone. The police department is well equipped to help you in these cases. This will be a case to call 9-1-1 before you do anything else. Remember the thought process back in response? Get the cavalry coming quickly; you can always send them back if you don't need them. Now some folks will say, "hey some kids write on the bathroom wall and you call the police?" Yes, it is still a threat and we make defendable decisions based on student safety. A threat is still a threat and the police investigate those. That is a *very* defendable decision.

This scenario starts with how you receive the threat. Usually there are three different ways that schools receive threat: written inside the school, via telephone, and via social media. All three have different implications and may require different responses. We will use a telephone threat as the basis for our exercise. Your secretary receives a call saying that a bomb has been planted in the school and will explode today. She tries to keep the caller on the phone and trace the call, but the person hangs up.[1]

Now you remember the excellent advice you read in this great book about school incident command (you know the one you are reading right now!) and you call 9-1-1 and get the reinforcements headed your way. You have your planning chief call the district office to get some help out to you. Now the calls are made and the reinforcements are coming, what do you do now? The next big question is usually the evacuation question? Do you pull the kids out?

This question has a lot of possible answers, and there are a lot of different theories. First, be aware if your district has a policy regarding this. Some want you to evacuate immediately, while others leave the decision up to you. There are some things to think about when it comes to making this decision:

- What are the current weather conditions? Will the students be exposed to the elements for a long period of time outside?
- Is there a risk that they will be more exposed to violence if they are outside than if they are still in the school? (We will talk about secondary devices too.)
- Is it possible that the caller is a student and it's a nice spring day so they want to head outside for "high school recess?"
- Will the students being outside have an impact on the response from the local police agency?

All are great questions that you need to consider. If the weather conditions are clear and warm, and if they do not create a separate issue, you may well decide to have an orderly evacuation and take the students out of the building. This is a defendable decision and will work well. However, there are some things you need to do first.

Earlier you read a note about secondary devices. Unfortunately, todays criminals are tricky and often think about ways to inflict more damage. Someone who means to do your students harm may call in a threat just to get you to evacuate and get the kids outside where they will be out in the open and vulnerable to a larger-scale attack.

For this reason, you should send out a search team (from your operations section) to check the area where the students will be held during the evacuation. Check for unusual objects or items that have apparently been left outside, such as backpacks. If these things are present, do not evacuate to this area. Let the police check them out and further clear the area so that it is safe to go out there.

Once they clear the evacuation area, have an orderly evacuation. There is really no need to pull the fire alarm and rush outside. Just get the students out to the safe evacuation area as quickly and efficiently as possible. Remember our two priorities: know where the students are and that they are safe. Make sure as you dismiss you are having accountability taken and that they are all accounted for. Once outside, the police can help determine if dogs are necessary to clear the school and will help guide you from there.

However, we should look at what happens if the weather just isn't that conducive. Can you keep the students in and still be safe? The answer is yes. There are ways to minimize the potential risk of keeping them inside. Remember, it may be safer inside because all of your students are not gathered in one exposed area. First, lock the school down.

Why the lockdown? It maintains control right away. You know where the students are and can begin your planning with students in areas where they can easily be accounted for. One possible response now is to have your operations section search the common spaces in the school while it's on lockdown. They can check the cafeteria and hallways, the gym and other open spaces to see if there are any openly visible threats or suspicious packages.

This is a good time to use your internal communications strategy. Teachers will be wondering what's going on. Send them an email that notes that you received a vague anonymous threat and would like them to check their classrooms briefly to see if there is anything out of the ordinary. Remember, no one knows a classroom like the teacher who is assigned to it. It may take you twenty minutes to search a classroom for something out of place because you have no idea where things go or don't go. A teacher in half the time can easily see if something is out of place.

If they write back or call with a concern, then you can evacuate that classroom. Send the kids to one of the places that you have cleared like the auditorium. Then when the police come in to search, not only will they search the common spaces but will also be able to search the classrooms where some staff members have said that there might be an issue. It will take dogs far less time to search common spaces and a few classrooms than it will to clear the entire school one classroom at a time.

Part of the issues here revolve around those common spaces in your building. Access is an important part of your building security for a number of reasons, but during these times when handling bomb threats they are more important than ever. Part of your mitigation strategy for bomb threats should include making sure that all the possible open spaces in the school remain locked when not in use.

Rooms like the boiler room or HVAC rooms, the custodial closets, and any storage rooms should always remain locked. Then you can feel better that these spaces will not necessarily need to be searched too thoroughly for a device because they are not open to allow anyone to place a package in them.

When the police arrive, they will most likely call for a bomb dog to search your facility. Part of your planning branch should be organizing how the dog should search, developing a list, and providing a floor plan as well as make sure that the K-9 officer gets an escort from the operations branch. Why the escort? Because they will need keys to access any doors that are closed. If you evacuated to the outside of the school, prior to the dog's arrival you may well wish to have all the doors opened inside the school and left propped open so that dog may be taken "off lead" or off their leash to freely follow their nose. As long as there are no real civilians or students present, that should not be a problem. It will actually speed up the process.

If you are in lockdown, no need to worry about opening all the classroom doors that are occupied. You should, however, open the doors that are to evacuated classrooms where there are concerns as well as those common spaces. If your operations branch completed a preliminary search of the school, they should note where they had concerns and make sure that the planning team includes that on the floor plan that they give the officer.

There are also tons of questions out there about using portable radios during a bomb threat. According to the experts, there is relatively little data that supports the possibility of a detonation because someone used a small portable radio. This is one of the times when we use our cost-benefit analysis to see that it would really create a dangerous situation if we sacrifice our communications. Just make sure that your team members use common sense. If they discover a suspicious package, do not stand directly over the package and use the radio. Move away to an area where they can safely use the radio without fear of the package going boom!

Once the building has been cleared by the police, you can bring the students back in or clear your lockdown. Remember, parents will be calling and the news will likely be sitting outside watching your school. Make sure you district PIO is aware of the situation and helping you to develop your message of what happened and what you did to protect their children.

You may also notice that we did not discuss a plan for calling the parents while all of this was going on. The reason is simple: your priority right now is to make sure the students are safe, and taking time out to communicate with parents may take time away from making critical decisions. If the school is in lockdown, they will not be able to come get their children right now anyway, so the call may just create unnecessary panic.

It is common for people to be afraid of things like threats of mass violence. They have unfortunately become a more common part of the educational experience. Just remember that most real bombers do not give anyone a warning that they are going to create damage. They want to inflict as much damage as possible and would not alert you which could allow you time to thwart their plan. A bomb threat is usually designed to create chaos and panic, not actual injury or death. There are some criminals out there who just like to wreak havoc.

LESSONS LEARNED

- ICS is not just for use during emergencies; it is a great organizational tool for handling non-emergency event planning.
- Training by using the ICS to plan for events gives your ICS team exposure to their roles and responsibilities in a controlled environment so they are not trying to figure it out on their own during an incident.
- Begin every use of the ICS team with an organization chart so that you know what resources you need to address the incident or event.
- Develop an incident action plan that includes as many important aspects of what needs to occur during management of the incident.
- Always brief the entire team so that everyone is aware of what the overall plan is to meet the needs of the operation.
- At the end of the exercise or each time the ICS team operates, they need to debrief and discuss what went right, what went wrong, and what they could do to improve next time.
- Train as if someone's life depends on it because every time your team is called upon to manage an incident, your ICS team is responsible for the safety of all of the students in your school. Take that responsibility seriously.

NOTE

1 Check with your technology department or phone company about trace procedures that could be used as soon as you receive a call. They vary from state to state.

Chapter 14

It's All about Mind-Set

The beginning of every shift for the fire or police department anywhere around the world starts with a roll call. It is where critical information about public safety is provided to the police officers and firefighters who are tasked with protecting our lives during their turn on the watch. Normally as educators you may start your day thinking about the next state testing cycle or where you are in your teacher evaluations. How can you combine these two important habits to better prepare for your role as an incident manager?

"Situational awareness" is the term used in public safety to describe looking at the different conditions in the community that may impact a police or fire department's ability to respond to emergencies. As you become more comfortable in your newfound skills as an incident manager, you will begin looking at the news events and other issues differently. An incident manager in schools looks at how events both locally and nationally may impact your school.

The media is not only an important source of information and occasionally entertainment, but it can also add to the difficulties of managing activities in a school. If the media covers a rash of bomb threats that lead schools to close as they were investigated, the copycat syndrome may occur as other students around the country try to bring about the same result. Listening to the news with an ear for how your students may respond to news events becomes an important tool in your incident management toolbox.

As you start your workday, look at things like the weather and how it could impact the school day. A thunderstorm forecast may bring the possibility of a power failure or a rapid onset of wind storm. Are your staff members prepared for the possibility? Perhaps sending the staff a quick note reminding them of how they should respond may be good ways to kick start their school day thinking about safety.

The habit of preparing mentally for an emergency is a mind-set that you should encourage your entire ICS team to adopt. Some educators focus on things such as cleanliness and stop to pick up trash and make sure the grounds are perfect. That is certainly important, but those things will not help when there is an emergency and your team has to manage it. They should pull up to the school and ask themselves, what can cause us a problem today and what can I do to prevent it?

These are great habits and should be encouraged. Your ICS team should also be looking with an eye toward things that may create an unsafe condition during the school day. As they walk past fire extinguishers mounted on the wall, they should occasionally stop and look at the extinguishers. Does the gauge show that the extinguisher is full? If they look at the horn where the product comes out, is it blocked by trash that some freshman thought would be cool to shove inside a fire extinguisher? Again, this is part of having the mind-set of preparing for any emergency.

Be observant and think about what could happen instead of what has happened or what is scheduled to happen. Part of your preparedness strategy is looking for things that may make it harder to handle an emergency or worse yet, could cause one! That means walking down the hall looking and actually seeing things that may be a problem.

Being observant can also be critical for not only natural disasters but also for man-made issues. Your staff member sees a parent walking down the hall looking into classrooms and looking irritated. They notice that the parent doesn't have a visitor pass around his or her neck or on the lapel. The staff member tries to ask the parent if he or she can help only to be rebuffed and told that the parent can find his or her son without the teacher's help.

The staff member calls the office from the nearest phone only to find out that the parent just lost custody of the child and indeed they never went to the office. The office alerts the school resource officer and principal who intercept the wayward parent and stop the situation before it becomes a true emergency. All because a staff member was paying attention!

We all have very busy maintenance people and custodians in our schools all of the time. These professionals are often focused on the job at hand and sometimes may miss little things that could impact school safety. For instance, if they are working in a ceiling and some wires are hanging down in the hallway, could this hamper your students' egress during an evacuation? Look at what they are doing and decide if it requires your team to add some thought? Maybe check in and see how long they will be working. If it's all day, then maybe a quick note to the team letting them know would be helpful.

KNOW YOUR SCHOOL

Yet another aspect of mind-set is knowledge about your facility. Everyone on your team should know the basics about how your school works. Is it heated with gas or electrical units? If it is gas, where are the gas shutoffs outside of the school? What about hazardous chemicals? Do you have a pool in the school? Then what is the possibility that you may handle an emergency in the pool area? The team should know where the pool chemicals are stored as well as where the MSDS (material safety data sheets) are located for the school. These sheets explain what hazard and risks are associated with the chemicals in the school as well as how to handle the emergency if the chemicals are released or someone sustains an injury involving them.

It is easy to say that the chief custodian and the operations folks will be there to handle things like fuel shutoffs and where the sprinkler or standpipe connection is located for your school, but remember incident command is about preparing for any possible contingency. What if they are engaged in another operation such as clearing the school? Would you have them stop to show the fire department where to connect to the standpipe? No, you would have another member of the ICS team show them so that the operations folks can continue what they are doing. That is why we cross train everyone for every position in ICS and make sure they are all familiar with the school.

LIFE SAFETY SYSTEMS IN YOUR SCHOOL

By the way, before you check the glossary or Internet to see what a sprinkler or standpipe is, let's review that part of our school. We should also become at least a little familiar with what the fire department or other agencies may do when they show up to help. That means knowing what resources are in your school that they will need to use.

If you look up above your head and see little metal disks about every six feet in the ceiling, your school is most likely sprinklered. Those devices are called sprinkler heads, and they work in a few different ways. There are separate pipes all through your school that are used only for sprinkler systems. Those pipes are always filled either with water or with compressed air. That tells you whether you have what is called a "wet or dry" system.

If your school has a wet system, then the pipes are all filled with water all the time. The way a sprinkler head works is sort of like a heat detector. There is a small tube called a fusible link, which is made of glass and a metal material that melts under certain temperatures. When the fire starts and the area above the fire reaches the temperature to melt the link, it breaks the bulb and allows the water in the pipe to come down and get distributed in a dome shape by that disk that you see in the ceiling. Normally only one or two sprinkler heads melt and begin to extinguish the fire or keep it from moving too far inside the school.

There are a few problems with these types of systems. One they can be used only if it is warm enough in the entire building not to ever freeze. If the pipes freeze, then there would be a blockage in the water flow and they may not work properly. The other problem that is common is that they can leak. Normally just a little leak here and there as the pipes are always under some type of pressure. This is not life-threatening but is a nuisance and can have your custodial crew going crazy replacing wet ceiling tiles!

The other type of system is the dry pipe system. In this case there is usually a compressor somewhere in the school in a room called the "sprinkler room." This is generally away from other parts of the boiler room because it keeps it separate from possible sources of fire. The compressor pumps compressed air into the sprinkler pipes, and there is enough pressure to keep a valve called the "check valve" closed, thus keeping water from flowing into the sprinkler pipes.

The sprinkler heads function the exact same way. When a fire starts under them, the fusible link breaks and the bulb shatters letting the air that is trapped in the line to escape. This release of pressure also releases the check valve, which then allows the water to flow to the sprinkler heads that activated. This type of system is very common in cold climates or where the entire school is not heated. The benefit is less water leaks. There are, however, more moving parts so more things that can go wrong. Sometimes the compressor malfunctions and your alarm company tells you that you have a "water flow" alarm. That just means that there was not enough air pressure and the check valve let water flow into the system. This is *not* an emergency but something that has to be addressed because if it is not repaired and the pipes freeze, you may encounter the same issues we reviewed with the wet system.

In both of these cases there is also an outlet outside of your school called the sprinkler connection. This allows the firefighters to hook up larger pressure and volume hoses to further support the sprinkler system. This will add water to the system and help put the fire out or keep it from moving until they can get real hoses in the room that is on fire.

Then there is that "standpipe" thing. You probably remember in the older schools that there was a fire cabinet on some of the hallway walls that you looked in and it had a fire hose and small nozzle all coiled up on a roller arm and a big rotating valve. It worked just like the hose at home, open the cabinet and pull the hose out and turn the valve to start fighting the fire. (The reason these are mostly gone now is that we want you to worry about kids and not be firefighters!) There is usually another connection in that cabinet to allow firefighters to hook their hoses up to it and fight the fire.

Schools do not have nearly the water capacity that a fire engine has. That fire engine can usually pump up to 1,250 gallons of water per minute on a fire. In very large buildings the architect didn't want the firefighters to have to drag hose all through the school to get to the fire so they add large pipes through the school and create places where firefighters can go hook up their hoses close to the fire. This is especially true in high-rise buildings where it is not practical to run hose vertically up the stairs which keeps people from using them. On the outside of the school is a standpipe connection that allows the entire school to become an extension of the fire engine. Now they can pump their 1,250 gallons per minute to the school and at one of those connections inside the firefighters can put the fire out.

Now that you know the basics, where are all of these devices? Does your school have a sprinkler system, and if so, when was the last time it was inspected? How about a standpipe? Where are those connections, and did you include them on the floor plan you have for the fire department? Then the firefighters don't just have to walk down a hallway looking for the connections, but you can show them where they are! Great way to work together!

YOUR TEAM IS *ALWAYS* ON CALL

Once you trained your ICS team in their different roles and they are familiar with the ICS and your school and all its functions, you need to develop a plan for how they actively work with each other. What happens if one is out for the day? Say your planning section chief is out sick. Luckily, you trained a few extra folks on the team in his role. However, the time for them to be aware that they are assuming the role is not during the actual emergency. They should be aware before school starts that they are the planning officer for the day. Your employees generally send an e-mail or leave a message with someone in the office so that they can get a substitute or just to let someone know. They should make it a habit to also let their alternate know. Then when you call for the ICS team over the intercom, the alternate already knows that he or she is up to bat and will be thinking like your planning person.

It also means that they can spend the day thinking about the "what if's" of their role. Let's assume that they are the planning officer and it's a cold and windy day. They know that the students will not be able to really stay outside for a long period of time during an incident. Thinking about that in advance will help them prepare for whatever comes their way. If you experience an incident and the fire department tells you it may be an hour or more before you can get back inside, your planning officer already thought about issues like using buses to stay warm or to relocate or even to dismiss.

VISUALIZATION MIND-SET

We have all heard professional athletes who tell the story of just visualizing the ball going in the net or over the fence. There are millions of success gurus out there who teach you how to visualize yourself as rich and successful therefor bringing the forces of the world together to help make it a reality. You and your team should use the same concept!

When you visualize what a perfect response would be based on what the conditions are today, you are playing the game mentally before game time. You are preplanning but not on paper, only in your head. You are thinking about how you would respond so that when it actually happens you have already prepared for it and are ready to respond. Sort of the way your wife or husband has a fight with you mentally long before he or she ever says anything to you. You always lose the fight with your spouse because he or she fought it already and preplanned what you are going to say! The same concept applies to incident command. You are already ahead of the curve if you have already managed the incident in your head before the alarm ever sounds.

LESSONS LEARNED

- Pay attention as you go through your day to the things that may impact your ICS team. Look at the weather for possible issues not just what to wear.
- Everyone on the team should get to know every aspect of your school. Important things such as how the school's heating or cooling plant works can help during an emergency.
- The team should know where the life safety systems are in the school and how they work. Things like a sprinkler system and standpipe should be readily available for use by the fire department.
- The team should always be ready to assume their role in the ICS every day that they come to work. They should make it a habit of informing their alternate if they are out sick or out of the building.
- The time to find out that you are missing a critical ICS team member is *not* after the alarm sounds!

Chapter 15

Preparing for School Violence

Anyone who writes books about school safety in this day and age must unfortunately include information about how to prepare yourself and your staff for the possibility of violence in or around your school. While it is a sad commentary on our society that the term "active shooter" has become a frequently heard phrase on the news involving students in schools, it is a reality and we should address it.

One of the first things that you should address as the school leader is the possibility that an act of violence could occur in your school. Many principals and teachers spend their career in a false sense of security because "it could never happen here." Rest assured in the small towns of America where seemingly safe and simple schools experience acts of terrible gun violence, their principal and staff believed the very same thing. While we can certainly hope that an event involving gun violence would never occur in our school, we should not be foolish enough to avoid preparing for it. In fact, it would be irresponsible for us not to consider the possibility.

As we consider the events involved in an active shooter situation, we should separate them slightly from the other events that we normally incorporate the incident command system. Historically an active shooter situation lasts less than ten to fifteen minutes. There is simply not enough time to actually implement your system especially given the fact that your team would have to move through the hallways to arrive at your command post and the threat exists in those same hallways.

WHAT IS WRONG WITH OUR LOCKDOWN?

For years we have focused our school emergency plans on locking our doors, turning out our lights, and hiding in closets or corners. There are a few problems with this concept. First is that it is simply well known and predict-able. Anyone who has attended a primary or secondary school in the past twenty years is familiar with lockdown procedures and can readily incorporate that in their assault plan. The second issue that comes to mind is the fact that this type of response is a passive response, a "hide and pray" type of response. It incorporates luck in hoping that the shooter will bypass your classroom or will be stopped before he or she comes to your room. It does not allow for staff members and students to take positive steps to ensure their survival.

This can be a difficult subject to discuss, but reality in today's world is simply that we must find ways to take positive steps to save our lives and the lives of our students when confronted with an armed intruder. They are bent on causing as much violence and death as possible in the shortest time span before (usually) taking their own life rather than being confronted by arriving law enforcement. They will use whatever means necessary to gain access to new targets, so simply locking the door that has a glass window, even with a curtain in it so they cannot see inside, may not stop them. One bullet to glass or even the stock of a rifle can shatter glass and allow them access.

WHAT CAN WE DO INSTEAD?

Instead you should work with your staff (with guidance from your local police department and your district office) to train your staff in methods to respond immediately to a hostile armed intruder in your school. There are many different systems out there to help school personnel prepare for this devastating incident. While each of these systems has some advantages and disadvantages, for the purposes of this book, we will review one of the earlier versions that is easy to learn and just as easy to apply.

The system is simply called "Run, Hide, Fight," and the name pretty well covers what you and your staff should think about doing in order of priority. We will review each step for some of the tips that will help your staff in pre-paring in advance for implementing this system while protecting themselves and their students.

WHAT DOES "RUN" LOOK LIKE?

Run means just that, if you can possibly escape outside of the school where the threat exists, go for it. If you are on the first floor and a shooter is coming down the hall, lock the door then either open a window or break the window with a chair or other objects so that you can send students outside and away from the shooter. Once outside, have them run toward the nearest place for cover, objects such as houses, and so on that would protect them from bullets if the shooter started shooting after them.

One of the questions that we as teachers frequently ask is, how do we get students to run in a line or do we walk? What if they scatter? The answer to that is simple: just keep them running and if they scatter, that's OK. The police and surely their parents would much rather you say that their children got lost in a neighborhood than that they were the casualty of a shooter. With all of the commotion being directed at the school, neighbors will likely come out and be able to help students get away. If you can keep them together, great. Once you are sure you are safe and away from the violence, call 9-1-1 from your cell phone or ask a neighbor to call 9-1-1 and tell the dispatcher what the location of the class is and if you have all of the students assigned to your room. The dispatcher can inform the police incident commander who will send someone to assist the class.

If you are simply in an area close to where the shooter is, just run away as far as possible and take as many turns as you can during your run. Why the turns? Because it will be better if the shooter is not looking straight at you and your students while you are running. The rule of thumb is simple here: if they can see you, they can shoot you. Get as far as you can from the shooter, and if you cannot escape out of the school, look for the place where you will enter into the "hide" phase.

A DEADLY VERSION OF HIDE AND SEEK

One thing about "hide" in this case is different from traditional hide and seek; we do not just hide in a closet and pray. Hide means to hide in a space where the shooter cannot find and access you. Just going into a closet or a bathroom is not going to be good enough. "Hiding" means making sure the shooter cannot find and access you. You want to make it hard for him or her to get into the room you are hiding in.

We need to keep in mind the nature of these events. The shooters know as soon as they fire the first shot, the good guys are coming. They look for quick and easy targets. If you make it hard for them to get into the room, they will move on to the next easy target. Remember they are cowards and are not trying to work hard; they want to shoot people who are easy to shoot.

In this option you need to find a way to hide your students in a target "hardened" room as best as you can. Remember these things are usually over in just a few minutes; the coward with the gun is generally trying to get as many casualties as quickly as he or she can. If you make it difficult for the shooter to access you and your students, he or she will most likely move to the next room.

Also making it hard for them to get to you has the added benefit of keeping them from hurting someone else while they try to defeat whatever you put in place to stop them from reaching you. You have two real goals when deciding where to barricade yourself. You need to think about places you can secure and places where the shooter will have the reduced chance to see you. If the door is locked and they cannot see in the room, they might move on looking for more accessible targets.

The ease of locking the door is a major concern as well as how easy it is to stay locked. Even if you cannot lock the door the old-fashioned way, there are other things that you can try to secure the door. If the door opens toward the inside, then you can use desks and other furniture in the room to block the door and keep the intruder from coming in.

If the door opens to the outside, even something like using an electrical cord or even a belt to wrap around the handle and from alongside the wall pull as hard as you can. This will create resistance and keep the shooter outside of the classroom. This can be especially helpful if the shooter cannot see inside. If you are in a high school classroom, get the strongest students to help hold the cord or belt. This is their survival too. Keeping quiet in the room is critical as well. Try to create the illusion for the shooter that the room is empty and locked. Remember their goal is as much damage in as little time as possible so if they think there is nothing, they will move on.

It is also important to limit the amount of noise or movement in the room. Make sure you silence cell phones because even on vibration they may attract unwanted attention. Try to keep everyone calm and quiet until the threat passes. You want them to move along to the next target, away from your classroom and the students you are protecting.

Keep the door closed, barricaded, and secured until you hear whatever release announcement or are rescued by the police. You have no guarantee that the threat is not still right outside a door, so don't risk it. Unfortunately, it is not worth the risk, stay locked, stay quiet, and stay safe.

THE LAST RESORT

So you are in a classroom, and there is no real way to barricade or secure the door. This is the very last stage of "Run, Hide, Fight." It is also you fight for survival. You must mentally prepare yourself to confront the shooter that is coming into your classroom intent on doing you and your students harm.

Look around your classroom. You may not have a weapon, but you can surely use the objects around you as an improvised defensive weapon. Furniture, books, fire extinguishers, or even a desktop computer can be used to throw at an attacker and attempt to injure or further stop the threat to your lives.

There is a lot of debate as to whether we should train students to fight. This is a hotly contested topic, and for the purpose of this book, we will only say that it is up to you and your district. That being said, in a genuine life-threatening crisis where there is a person shooting and trying to kill you, every able-bodied person who can fight may need to fight. A class of high school students can throw objects at an attacker more effectively than one lone teacher! As we said in the hide section, it is their life on the line as well as your own!

Your next step should be to determine whether the shooter is down and if he or she is no longer any threat to you and your students. If it's at all possible, disarm the attacker and flea as quickly as possible with your students. If that's not possible, continue to attack until you're assured that there's no longer a threat to you and your students. If you do happen to take a weapon away from the shooter, make sure that you don't carry it in a threatening way in case you're confronted by the police. You may want to simply get rid of it as quickly as possible but far away from the attacker. When you do meet with the police, let them know where the attacker is and where the weapon is.

Don't worry about disarming the attacker if there's a possibility of escaping as quickly as possible. Use the element of surprise and eliminate the threat, but your job is to protect yourself and your students and not to worry about anyone else. They will all have to fend for themselves. So if you're able to surprise the attacker and give yourself and your students an opportunity to escape, take advantage and quickly get away from the threat.

I hate to make this seem so dire, but these are our unfortunate realities. In fact, corporate America has had to embrace incidents such as these which could occur in a shopping mall, restaurant, or even in a church. There are really no safe places where you do not have to think about what you would do if confronted with a horrific act of gun violence.

It is important to think about these things in your classrooms well before the event occurs. Unfortunately, this is not the time to begin thinking about what you will do if there is a person with a weapon in your school after you hear the first shots. Then certainly there will be some amount of panic, and you will have to do what you can to give yourself and your kids the best chance to survive.

Your body has a physiological response to a threat and panic. If you begin to breathe heavily and your heart rate increases, you will notice that you start to get "tunnel vision" as the oxygen level in your brain and your optic nerves decreases. This is because your body will try to survive by bringing blood back into your central core toward the heart. Try using what we call "tactical breathing" which is to inhale for three or four seconds, hold it for three or four seconds, and blow it out for three or four seconds. That will help you keep your head and thoughts (and vision) clear.

The same thought occurs in any stressful situation, so it's a good tool to use if you are confronted by your teenager coming home three hours late for their curfew! Try it, it works!

These are just a few thoughts. Consult with your district office as well as local police agency or state school safety office to look at training in the area of active shooter response and safety. This small amount of information does not replace a good training program, and there are hundreds of good books focused exclusively on surviving an active shooter, even some focused on schools exclusively.

It is unfortunate that there has to be something that we all address in schools, but this is a book about being prepared for any eventuality so we must consider any possibility. Those who work with children today must unfortunately remember that they are occasionally a target for an armed person with mental health issues. As we said in the chapter on planning, it means doing a realistic threat and risk assessment. That must include the worst-case scenario.

LESSONS LEARNED

- Just locking down without any other plan is called sitting duck; we cannot afford to just lock the doors and hope for the best.
- Always think "Run, Hide then Fight."
- The key is to act quickly and escape if possible. If you can get the students outside and away from the violence, go for it.
- Once outside get them behind something as you escape; this will conceal them and protect them from possible gunfire.
- If you cannot run, then you hide. That means barricading your door and creating as many obstacles as possible for the shooter to breach to get to you and your students.
- As a very last resort, be prepared to fight.
- Anything can be a weapon, from a textbook to a fire extinguisher. Look around your room regularly to see what you would use to defend yourself against a threat.
- Always think "what if." What would you do to escape if you were somewhere in school and something happened?
- This is not about a planning checklist, but it's about a survival mentality.

Glossary

- **Accountability**: The primary goal of the school-based incident command team is to ensure that all students are located and accounted for as well as to ensure their safety.
- **Active Shooter Incident**: An incident in which an armed intruder enters a school and begins firing his or her weapons in an attempt to injure or murder the students and staff of the school.
- **Command Post**: The room or location used during an incident or an emergency where the incident command team meets to develop an action plan and manage the resources and staff needed to respond to an incident or an emergency.
- **Emergency**: Situation involving an immediate threat to the welfare and safety of the students and staff of your school.
- **Emergency Management Cycle**: Breakdown of the four phases that are required to create, implement, and operate an effective emergency and incident management program. The phases are mitigation, preparedness, response, and recovery.
- **Fire Apparatus**: Equipment that responds with members of the fire department to emergencies. Generally, it consists of three different types of equipment: engines which use water to extinguish fires, ladder trucks which are responsible for rescuing trapped students and staff as well as ventilating the hazardous gasses associated with a fire, and rescue trucks which are equipped with specialized equipment and trained firefighters who can manage difficult technical rescues as well as assist in firefighting efforts.
- **Incident**: A situation that impacts and hampers the ability of the staff and students of the school to continue the learning process without interruption.
- **Incident Action Plan**: The plan developed by the planning section chief and approved by the incident commander that designates tasks that should

be performed by operations section staff members to help manage the incident or emergency. The action plan also determines what resources the logistics section needs to procure in order to implement the objectives of the plan. It does not need to be a formal document, but it is imperative that all ICS team members are aware of the plan and acting in accordance with it.

- **Incident Command Facilities**: Locations on your school property that are used for a specific purpose during an incident or an emergency. These facilities include the command post, the reunification center, and the staging area.
- **Incident Command System**: System which uses common language and breaks down roles and responsibilities of staff members in order to effectively manage an incident or an emergency. ICS is an organizational tool that can be used to organize activities and personnel in order to more effectively manage an incident. The system is expandable from one single person using it to break down tasks to several hundred staff members and resources managing a large-scale incident or emergency. System is used by public works and public safety agencies uniformly across the country. For this reason, the terminology and roles are universal across different agencies with different responsibilities. It allows all of those agencies to respond together effectively.
- **Incident Commander**: Person who assumes overall responsibility for the management of incidents and emergencies that occur in your school. The incident commander (or IC for short) is the leader of the school incident command team and is usually the principal.
- **Life Safety Systems**: The systems installed in a school designed to create an early warning of a hazardous condition as well as designed to quickly reduce the possible impact of an emergency. Fire and smoke alarms as well as sprinkler systems are examples of life safety systems which should be in place and maintained in *all* schools.
- **Lockdown**: The act of securing the school, either internally or externally, in an effort to create multiple barriers between the students and people who pose a possible threat to their safety.
- **Logistics Section Chief**: The person in the ICS Command Staff who works with the planning section chief to determine what resources are needed to manage an incident or an emergency. They are responsible for making recommendations to the incident commander and managing the resources that are sent to the scene. Logistics also manages the staging area facility used to stage equipment and staff until needed at an incident.
- **Mitigation Phase**: The first phase in the emergency management cycle that involves looking at what potential risks and hazards exist at your school

and creating an effective plan for reducing those risks and responding to those incidents.

- **Operations Section Chief**: The person in the incident command system who manages the resources and staff that physically perform tasks during an incident or emergency. The operations section implements the plans approved by the incident commander.
- **Planning Section Chief**: Person in the ICS who is responsible for the short- and long-term planning during an incident or emergency. They look at the incident right now and set goals and objectives for managing the incident as it progresses. One of the three section chiefs who make recommendations and report to the incident commander.
- **Preparedness Phase**: The second phase of the emergency management cycle. After the plan is created, the preparedness phase is about the day-to-day activities that are undertaken to reduce the risks of an emergency occurring or find ways to help reduce the possible impact of an incident or an emergency. This is the normal day-to-day phase that your school and ICS team are in every day until it is time to respond to an incident or an emergency.
- **Public Information Officer**: The person from the school or district who is responsible for communicating with the media regarding a particular incident or emergency. Should be someone who is not actively involved in managing the ICS to allow them to focus on developing the incident action plan and its implementation.
- **Recovery Phase**: This is the phase of the emergency management cycle that occurs after the team has successfully responded to and managed an incident or an emergency. During this phase the equipment and resources that were used to manage the incident are repaired and readied for the next possible incident. Any repairs to the school are made during the recovery phase. The mental health and welfare of the staff and students after an incident are addressed as well during this phase. The recovery phase is considered complete when the school and staff are ready to return to the normal day-to-day learning environment. If there is no need to change the school's emergency response plan after an incident, the school's team returns to the mitigation phase and prepares itself for the next incident or emergency.
- **Response Phase**: This is the phase of the emergency management cycle where you and your staff are actually responding to an incident or an emergency. During the response phase you will utilize the incident command system to more effectively manage the incident or emergency.
- **Reunification Center**: This location is a secure location set up when parents are being asked or permitted to pick up their children from an incident or emergency. This location should allow clerical staff to review IDs

and information to ensure that students are released only to the appropriate people. Students are kept physically away from this location until the staff is able to determine that the student can safely be released.

- **Run, Hide, Fight**: A priority-based decision-making system designed to be used during an active shooter event which stresses getting away from the threat, securing yourself out of the path of the threat, or engaging the threat in aggressive action designed to save the lives of staff and students.
- **Staging Area**: The location managed by the Logistics Section where resources and staff that are not immediately needed at the scene of the incident are located and standing by until they are needed on the scene. This keeps down the congestion and chaos at the scene. The staging area can be on the property or a short distance from the scene but must be quickly and efficiently accessible for a quick response by these resources.
- **Tabletop Exercise**: A training session involving the incident command team discussing possible incidents or emergency scenarios and assuming their roles in the ICS to plan how they would respond to and manage the incident or emergency.

About the Author

Brian N. Moore is the supervisor of Public Safety for the Red Clay Consolidated School District in Delaware. He has written multiple articles on school safety and emergency management for several national education journals. He has presented numerous workshops around the country to help districts and schools prepare for emergencies. In addition to having been a Reserve Police Officer, Brian was a volunteer firefighter and instructor for more than twenty years. He served as a fire chief and emergency manager for a marine transportation company prior to joining the District. He has been an outspoken advocate for safer schools. In his home state of Delaware, Brian was a subject matter expert hired by the state Department of Safety and Homeland Security to help develop and roll out a comprehensive school safety plan that was later required by law to be adopted in every public school in the First State.

Brian holds a master's degree in business administration with a specialization in homeland security from Wilmington University. In addition to his work in schools, Brian teaches English and Communication at the Delaware Technical and Community College. He served as the Chairman of the Editorial Board for School Business Affairs magazine for several years. Brian has been a member of the Board of Directors of the Police Athletic League of Delaware for more than a decade and is a strong advocate for programs that help at-risk youth to reach their potential in life.

Brian lives with his wife of twenty-five years Karen and their children Brendan and Megan Moore in Greenville Delaware.

Made in United States
North Haven, CT
28 August 2023

40853029R00088